Snapshot of a
Warped Man

MICHAEL SHASHOUA

LIBRARY OF CONGRESS CATALOGING-IN-PUBLICATION DATA

Names: Shashoua, Nathan Michael, author

Title: Snapshot Of A Warped Man / Michael Shashoua

[236 pages]

U.S. Copyright Office registration number TXu 2-382-726 / TXu002382726

Identifiers:

Library of Congress Control Number: 2023919396

ISBN paperback 979-8-218-27437-5
ISBN ebook 979-8-218-27438-2

Disclaimer

Events depicted in this book are the author's memories from his perspectives. Some names have been changed or last names omitted to protect identities of those involved.

Subject: Memoir

Printed in the United States

Published by Nathan Michael Shashoua in Plainsboro, N.J.

www.facebook.com/SnapshotWarpedMan

Contents

Prologue

This is a journey through a life that got fucked up, not through high drama but through inevitable quiet consistency. It got that way as psychological, social and emotional letdowns accumulated. On this warped foundation, I built a tower of shame and guilt. It never toppled, just stood crooked.

Some names will be changed to protect the innocent and the unwitting accomplices.

Time after time, I never quite connected with the world around me or the people in it. There were a few other kids my age in the neighborhood, but I wasn't close with any of them and mostly did my own thing. I'd pedal around the driveway in a toy fire engine, dig around in the dirt in the backyard flower bed, and later make up games and imaginative creations in my head to play on my own or draw or write about.

Our house was a one-story ranch in a suburb of Trenton, N.J., down the lane from a poorer Black neighborhood, yet further away from the richer neighborhoods. The house had a concrete foundation and basement and light green horizontal siding. To play catch, I bounced tennis balls off the garage door, chipping off pieces of the siding when my throws missed.

On rare occasions, my sister and I would run around with two or three other kids in the neighborhood. They'd come to us or we'd roam down the street to them. It wasn't often enough to remember their names or stay friends with them once we were in school or camp elsewhere. My parents and my grandma who lived with us left us alone. We were free to play unsupervised, which was normal in the 1970s and 80s.

Computers would figure a lot in my life later on. We were late adopters of the Atari home video game console, but early to get an Apple II-e computer, which had a green on black monitor to show text and some primitive graphics. Before hermetically sealed Macs came along, the II-e let you install the memory cards yourself. I was so proud that I could do the set-up. We kept it in a basement corner office sectioned off with paneling. Later, I'd spend hours there learning to touch type and playing a Dr. J-Larry Bird video basketball game. I was in the first generation that devices started to keep kids from playing outside.

But that isolation wasn't absolute yet. I'd get out to a basketball court at a nearby grade school, or ride my bike around our neighborhood.

The earliest stirring of sexual simulation came from the 1970s TV version of "Wonder Woman" with Lynda

Carter. I must have been at most six or seven years old, and I didn't understand what was happening when my penis got hard. There weren't other kids around to ask, so I asked my mom about it. She didn't know what to say, but kept a straight face. I don't remember her response to the question.

Plugging the Hole With A Baseball

The home where all this happened was my first home, from birth to age 15. The floors were bare wood, before the next house where we had carpet. One of my earliest memories is of a rainbow circle that would form on the living room wall opposite the front door from a prism created by the glass peephole. My sister and I got fascinated with this. We'd stand on the couch, examine it, and play by covering up parts of the circle rainbow. We were easily amused.

There was a low brown coffee table, that now still sits in a storage locker. There we each had our designated spaces for little piles of magazines, papers or toys. There was a set of two brown upholstered chairs and a couch with uncovered wooden arms and legs. My father was sitting on one of those chairs the last time I saw him in the morning before he died, in late January 1982. This is one of many memories that I blocked out but which came back later in full. I must have been misbehaving that morning before leaving for school, and he complained with anger and frustration, "Do you want me to be sick?" He had a heart attack or attacks before, and heart issues for the past three or four years. Just about a month before my 10th birthday, those were the last words I heard him say.

I remember viewing dad in his coffin in the low-lit chapel of the local funeral home. Leaning in, I saw my dad's face with his eyes closed, his expression blank and his soul gone. It's a fleeting memory, one I can only barely picture now, more as an idea than the event itself. I must have begun crying and was led away, but I don't know or recall for sure. And I don't remember the funeral service or the burial. I must have blocked it all out afterward, subconsciously not wanting to remember the pain of him dying and being buried.

After my dad's cardiac issues started, we would get Egg Beaters egg substitute for him to eat. Real eggs were bad for him, or so it was thought then. My overbearing grandma on my mom's side of the family lived with us, and she would raise tensions and pick arguments with my dad. After one of these, Dad sat in the basement on a beat up wide chair with frayed pine green upholstery, by himself, with his head in his hands.

Months after he passed, I dreamt that I found him sitting in that chair in the basement. I was excited, showing off my baseball card collection to him, including a card I'd just got autographed through the mail by star spitball pitcher Gaylord Perry. I knew or remembered that my dad loved baseball. When he got to the U.S. as a teen from Iraq, he went to Yankees games as a way to

6

Americanize himself. It was said that he'd seen both Joe DiMaggio and Mickey Mantle play.

After my dad passed, I got more interested in baseball. I hadn't been old enough to be close to my dad before he passed. Again, subconsciously maybe I got into baseball because I knew he liked the game. I went on to play Little League and some youth baseball until I couldn't keep up with the other kids' skills. If my dad lived to see me quit baseball, we would have clashed about that, especially once it got compounded with teenage rebellion. If he lived to see me grow up, though, maybe we would have found common ground talking about the game, when I later became a fan again.

Baseball was the thing that filled the hole of my dad's absence. From ages 10 to about 13, I'd beg the neighbor across the street who had been friends with my dad to pitch wiffleballs to me on our lawn. I'd rope my sister in to playing wiffleball also. But baseball wasn't going to be enough to compensate for the loss by itself, especially after puberty hit.

A year after my dad passed, in the 1983 season, my mom took me to a live game for the first time – the Phillies at Veterans Stadium. She had grown up in Philadelphia, and we were closer to Philly than to New York, so we were Phillies fans. The Phils were in a rare period of regular playoff appearances, with a 1980 World Series win and a Series loss at the end of that 1983 season. Playing baseball and being a Phillies fan was a big part of my life as a kid for a long while, until I discovered rock music.

Faith Upended

I went to kindergarten at the local public school, but then my sister and I went to a Hebrew day school in Trenton. There it was decided that I was smart enough to skip first grade, but not for the Hebrew studies which were completely new to me. So halfway through each day, I remember having to separate from the first graders and join the second graders, a little kid overwhelmed by hallways filled with all the kids bigger than me as I had to find my way through them to a different classroom. A first warping.

When I entered fifth grade, the year my father died, the school moved to a historic, handsome old school- house building across the river in Yardley, Pa. I was one of the first students at the Yardley location, which after 40 years is now multiples larger in size and numbers of students.

At the Trenton location, we'd carpool in with our Ewing neighbors, whose daughter also went there. A small

Orthodox synagogue owned the two-story building but just used a small portion on the first floor. It had a fenced in blacktop pavement playground area that seemed vast to a little kid, but was not even a whole block. There was just enough room to play kickball in the blacktop yard.

On the drive in every morning, we'd see a gray-haired uniformed crossing guard who would smile and wave to us as we passed. One day, he pointed at me and said, "Your shoe's untied," and of course I looked down even though I was inside the car. I'm envious now that he came up with something that funny. The element of surprise in a well-executed joke like that delighted me. When I'm quick enough to surprise someone, even with an inside joke, it's satisfying.

Once I settled in completely to one grade level and didn't have to switch classrooms, in Trenton, and later in Yardley, I became gregarious, even a little obnoxious. A few of my friends out of the class of 10 or so in our grade were from richer households, but one was also from Ewing and more down to earth.

This distinction got more concrete after fifth grade in the new location. The only reason I stayed in the school through eighth grade, even though we couldn't afford the tuition, was his passing. A few weeks before he died, he had complained at a parents' meeting about the higher tuition in Yardley. The rabbi who ran the school felt bad and gave us a free ride scholarship for the rest of our time there. That still didn't stop me from rebelling in seventh grade.

I couldn't articulate my grief and anger at my dad's passing. It found its way out through teenage rebellion, then depression in college and as a young adult. I wasn't capable of mourning as a child and these were manifestations of not having mourned.

I learned later that my dad himself grieved before he died, because he knew he wouldn't live to see my Bar Mitzvah. My mother told me that 30-plus years later when her cancer relapsed terminally. I hadn't had the presence of mind, then, to think of all the questions I might have wanted to ask her and things I wanted to know. She'd been open to try to answer anything I might have asked. I regret that I lacked enough sense of the moment to take her up on this. There were other details I got at other times though. A story about my mom and dad going to do something in New York that he insisted on – a show or a nice dinner – and he was too out of breath to walk more than a block at a time without stopping. So the cardiac issues he had were affecting other aspects of his health too.

Another facet of going to the Hebrew day school once it moved into Pennsylvania was long bus rides. We lived only about 15 minutes away, but the bus picked us up early and dropped us off last in the afternoons. An older kid on the bus, Robert, egged on wrestling matches between me and a younger kid, Golan, who was still bigger and stronger than me. How the driver didn't put a stop to these, I have no idea. This shouldn't have been happening, especially at a private religious-based school that claimed to have a higher purpose.

I wanted to tell some adult that this was happening, but I was afraid to do that – thinking it would make it worse if I got my tormentor in trouble. Eventually, feeling upset and demeaned by what was going on, I did tell somebody and they must have talked to Robert, and it stopped. I'd also been trapped into thinking that I should fight and prove myself, but I was overmatched.

That was one of the first times I remember feeling inferior and down on myself. I wasn't quite a teenager yet. It's significant as the start of the slide for my personality, down to quiet moodiness. This was an incident that unlocked the effects of not having a father around.

I wasn't as studious as my sister, but I was diligent in school and later at training for my Bar Mitzvah. Learning the tropes to read the Torah aloud gave me pride and satisfaction. I could memorize the tropes to recite the scroll without the cheat sheet guide that added those to the text. At the same time, though, I'd get filled with anxiety about elementary school spelling tests (in English). I'd run through those vocabulary lists over and over again while trying to go to sleep.

After my Bar Mitzvah, though, I dropped out of Jewish studies and Jewish social groups. Having to sing Hebrew songs in an NCSY group setting seemed corny to me. The teenage desire to seem "cool" took hold. I felt embarrassed and square about the Jewish stuff, rather than proud. I was on my way out of the Hebrew day school and on to secular public high school anyway.

I wanted to be in the secular world. I was getting into rock and pop music, going through puberty and wanted to be with girls but had no idea how. Still, I was pursuing my own interests – writing, pop culture, movies and TV, literature, etc. I was becoming my own person, not one ruled by religion. My mom didn't force it on me once the Bar Mitzvah and Hebrew school were done. Fulfilling what my dad wanted me to complete was enough, I guess. Despite moving away from the religion on purpose, enough of it stuck that I'd sometimes turn to it, and eventually wanted to pass it on.

When I found myself in unfamiliar territory, I'd go back to religion. It wasn't like I suddenly became a believer, but I needed community and a support system. At times, I got lost and scared in new surroundings, like when I took jobs in Pennsylvania and Florida in my 20s.

I knew all the melodies for all the prayers at services and could pick them up again without a thought. These were so ingrained in my mind, I'll never forget them. You could drop me into a synagogue anytime and I could jump right into the recitation, chanting or singing. What once was embarrassing became a comfort.

I'd still join a temple in unfamiliar surroundings, even carrying so much doubt. I'd think, "How could God take away my dad as a kid and make me suffer like I did?" I didn't buy the typical answer to a complaint like that, which isn't unique to Judaism. Clergy would say that God works in mysterious ways and people are too simple to understand the deity's greater plans for their lives.

I operated with a split personality, being diligent about taking part in synagogue services even as hormones and thoughts about girls began to bubble up in me, but then abruptly dropping all the Jewish activity after my Bar Mitzvah. As an adult, though, in other towns, after my sexual perversions had become habitual and a source of shame, I'd turned back to going to synagogue again, projecting the image of a good young man.

In Daytona, Florida, now age 26, I turned up for a Saturday morning service soon after getting diagnosed with depression and anxiety. During the Kiddush after services, a boisterous, heavy-set man in his later 50s with gray hair introduced himself. I happened to mention that my mom was from Philadelphia. It turned out that he was too. He took me under his wing right then for the entire time I was in Florida. I'd go for dinner and hang out with him and his family once a week, and we'd usually go see a movie. It was always a happy, lively and upbeat scene at his house, and that's the kind of guy he was. He embodied the spirit of welcoming the stranger in town, a Jewish ideal. Spending time with him and his family gave me a place to go enjoy myself once a week, something to look forward to, some connection or closeness with someone.

Discovering Music

I remember more about objects from when I was a child than I do about other kids. I can tell you more about the first vinyl 45s and albums that I bought than the names of other kids I played with in my neighborhood. Dropping the needle on "Private Eyes," I'd watch the completely black circle spin. The center was the black RCA Records label with silver printed type and the white RCA outline logo, making the whole disc mostly black. The edge of the single would move very slightly up and down. It seemed like the record was bouncing along with the drum and piano sound on the track.

The first two albums I got were "Synchronicity" by The Police and "Under A Blood Red Sky," a landmark live album from U2. A video of "Sunday Bloody Sunday" taken from the show at Red Rocks in Denver, had put U2 on the map and gotten my attention to go buy this live album.

The lyrics of these two records, especially Sting's literary references and intellectual aspirations, felt powerful and transcendent. I can't say I was a punk rock prodigy or got into harder rock music as a kid. I still liked a bit of polish on the music. I like music that sounds dynamic, grand and produced, and that was the case from the start.

At first, around ages 11 and 12, I played these records on our cheap Sears phonograph with junky speakers. I'd pour over the "Synchronicity" album cover and inner sleeve lyrics for hours. This evolved into a fetish for every piece of music packaging. If a vinyl album had a sticker on the shrink wrap advertising the hits on the album, I'd cut that out and keep it inside. Same thing with cassettes later. My rationale was that someday I'd need a way to know what songs on the albums had been promoted as singles. I'd go on to make lists and queues this obsessively all my life – Netflix queues of course, but also with porn videos and camgirls.

Weird Kid

At those ages – 10, 11, 12 -- there weren't the distractions kids have today, namely constant games and social media on phones. So I invented little imaginative games and made-up scenarios. These were specific and rigid. They required imagination but had a strict structure. As I'd bounce a tennis ball or rubber ball against that garage door, I'd pretend I was playing out the career of a baseball player. Every 10 throws was a season, and how many times I caught the ball would be how good the player was that season. I have no idea if any other kid in the history of childhood ever did anything like this – an imagined scenario but one with very specific boundaries. I'd get tired, and miss the catches more, simulating a pro baseball player's real decline over time.

We didn't have a basketball hoop when I was a kid. I lobbied for one sometimes. I played the same game in my head shooting baskets at the nearby elementary school court or at my cousin's house with a hoop in the driveway. Still pretending I was making the career of a baseball player, because I wouldn't make that many shots. Three out of 10, like a .300 batting average in baseball, would be pretty good.

At the beginning of the movie "40-Year Old Virgin" Steve Carell's character rides around on a bicycle, looking silly, for a while. It was a minute or two in the movie, but when the studio asked the filmmakers to show them footage while making it, they gave them 15 or 20 minutes of Carell riding the bike around, lost in his own world. Thus inhabiting the character very well, but not inspiring confidence from the studio. If someone watched me acting out my baseball scenarios, mumbling about made up stats under my breath, it must have looked a little like Carell on that bike.

I'd do this and wouldn't be playing with other kids. My daughter likes to make up pretend games in her head and dictate them to us or other kids to join in. I'm not surprised by that, remembering these games of my own. Hers seem more normal though, unbounded by some anal, obsessive rules.

My other imaginary game could be played indoors. When I got into music and began collecting full albums, I got a frame of reference for this game. I would imagine the career of a band or group, like my favorites such as Genesis, The Police, Peter Gabriel or U2. On index cards, I'd draw an album cover, with a made up name for the artist, a made up album title, made up song titles (without actually writing any real songs for those titles), and the names of the musicians. Each card would be an album. I'd create ways that the group or artist was changing from album to album. The next album card would show those changes. I'd end up with 10 cards for 10 albums by an imaginary band making stylistic shifts, like going from '70s progressive rock to pop, or punk to pop, or pop to acoustic stuff.

As age 11 turned to age 12, and age 12 turned to age 13, with puberty setting in during those years, I found, or invented, new games in my head. These were sexual fantasies mushed into game-like formats.

How Grandma Became My Porn Connection

The first step was getting sexy or suggestive pictures. I'd sneak around, trying to see magazines in the local Quick Chek without anyone noticing. I'd go down the second aisle in, where the magazine rack was. I'd stand there, pretending to look at some of the regular magazines, glancing from side to side. I'd have my eye on the Playboys on the top rack. When I was sure no one was watching, which is tough when people are coming in and out of a busy convenience store, I'd grab a Playboy off that top rack. I'd bring it down to the lower shelf to look through it without being detected. A game of evasion.

Another source back then was a publishers' overstock catalog that often came in the mail. It had a glossy cover and about 80 to 100 thin newsprint pages, like a thick magazine. I wasn't interested in its giant history tomes, romance novels or cheesy mysteries. But the back of the

21

catalog had titillating "art" photography books, like "The Art of Mud Wrestling."

How could I get my hands on that? Scheming, I thought I could get my grandma to write a check or a money order, while obscuring what it was actually for. I could say I wanted to get some of the history books from the catalog. This wasn't like when I asked mom to buy a Playboy when I was eight or nine years old. Then, I had no guile and didn't feel it was shameful. Now I wanted to keep this a secret. I felt like my desires were wrong and I didn't want to be embarrassed.

After school one day, I walked down the short hall to my grandma's bedroom. She kept to herself in there, watching TV, coming out sometimes to nag my sister and me about homework or chores. Grandma was particularly hard on Yvonne, and I never figured out why. I guess old school women of that generation were harder on young girls as a rule. I realized I could use the insight that grandma liked me better than my sister to my advantage. I worked up courage to lie, or bend the truth a little, and knocked on the door.

"Come in."

"Grandma, could you order a book for me?" I said, getting right to the point.

"What book?"

"A history book and a book about movies from a catalog. I'll do the order and mail it," I said, thinking making it easy for her might help get over for this. "It says check or money order for $13.95 plus shipping. Oh, shipping is $1.50, so it's actually $15.45. The check has to go to 'Publisher's Direct.'"

"Okay," she said. "Let me sit down and I'll write one for you."

She didn't ask any further about the titles of the books, a big relief since I hadn't thought of a decoy answer for that. I wondered for a second why a grown-up wouldn't ask more about what the money was for. I'd fooled her -- she had no idea, I assumed. But she must have known something was up and played along with my scheming to undermine my mom. There was a complicated history between my grandma and my mom, and between my grandma and my parents together as a couple. In short, grandma thought she should be or was in charge of us, and that her word should be law, even if my parents disagreed.

A few weeks later, I found myself thinking, *My book should be here soon. I better be on the lookout for it.* Thus began a new ritual. The mail would come before I got home from school around 3:30, or sometimes a little after that. Once it hit 14 days or so, like the catalog promised, I had to start watching out for the book. Every day as I got home from school, I'd look in the mailbox. If the mail was there, I'd bring it in, day after day. If it wasn't, I'd often look out the picture window for the mail truck, or to check if the mailbox flag was down.

After a couple weeks of this, longer than expected, I got home from school one day and grandma said, "There's a package for you." *This is it!* I thought, but then kicked myself for not catching it before anyone else knew a package arrived. I took the large padded envelope off the kitchen table and went to my room. Shutting the door, I pulled the thin hardcover book out. The cover showed three women in a kiddie pool with mud splattered all over them, grabbing at each other's bikini tops. I felt myself get hard as I flipped the pages, seeing the women posed in fights. They were clean at first, then got muddier on each page. Yet their hair stayed perfect, with the mud stopping at their necks, their faces still clean.

These images cast a spell that only broke when my grandma's yelling cut through, telling me it was time for snack. That yell shocked me as much as if she'd walked in the room and seen me aroused. "Oh shit," I thought. After I collected myself from that shock, I waited for my boner to go down, and then put the book in a box under my bed. It was that moment that started the fears of getting caught – and a determined effort to avoid being caught at this behavior no matter what.

*   *   *

I rehearsed how to ask my grandma for another money order, this time for a videotape I'd already rented once. I aimed to pattern my patter after the way I'd asked for getting the picture book. After several repetitions, I walked, step after deliberate step, down the hall to my grandma's room.

I recalled how exciting the tape was, and how I first saw it. I'd gotten a new bike that summer, after the old one got stolen from the local pool when I forgot to bring my bike lock. From all those times my mom drove me places, including the video store, I remembered how to reach them on a bike. There, I'd browse the racks of empty cardboard VHS boxes that reached up to the ceiling. I'd find the suggestive spring break comedies. The store had a curtained off adult video section that I didn't dare try to enter. Even standing face to face with the sexy VHS movies, my tension rose and I'd look sideways, hoping no one noticed me.

One day, desire at last superceded fear of embarrassment or at least any caring about what store clerks thought about me. I brought one of the boxes with a bikini girl on the cover up to the counter to rent. A bored college boy stood behind the counter, elevated a little, and took the box. I still couldn't look the clerk in the eye, that would be too embarrassing. I hoped he'd do the rental quick and not ask anything. To my surprise, that's exactly what he did. at was the easy part. How would I actually watch the tape?

The next day, I tried to see what would work. I sat on the living room floor, in front of the big console TV with the VHS player on top. The VCR remote plugged in with a cord that must have been seven feet long. Should I sit on the couch to the right so I could glance back down the hall to catch anyone coming out of the bedrooms? Or should I stay in this spot on the floor? I guessed that would block whatever I played on the TV for a couple seconds, giving me time to hit stop on the remote. I got up off the floor, and moved to the couch, seeing how that felt for being able to cover my viewing up. Then I moved back to the floor. The floor didn't seem as good for being able to see behind me or around me and react.

I got up again and laid down on the couch. I looked back down the hall again. I realized I forgot to turn the volume down on the TV. No remote for the TV, so I got up to turn the knob. Then back down on the couch again. I glanced back again. Tensing up, I pressed play.

The video started in a club where girls in bikinis danced around a blue plastic tarp-covered pit. Then came quick clips of the action that ran in full later in the video, showing these girls wrestling in oil and mud. I felt myself getting excited again. I looked back, checking again that no one was coming out into the room. Satisfied, I turned back to watch, getting harder as girls came out in pairs and started wrestling. Remembering where I was and that my grandma could come out at any time, I stopped to calm down. I was training myself in how to regulate my desire, to be able to get into the stimulation, but still be aware enough of what could be happening around me enough to shut it down and cover it up fast. It was no longer exactly or only a fear of being caught, or shame, but a cold calculation about how to maximize what was possible and minimize a bad outcome – being caught.

*   *   *

Watching the tape went on that way for a while. I got to be 14 or 15, when I found another avenue that went further with how explicit that content was. I was still getting those publishers catalogs, and noticed a few pages in the back had little ads for videos. These looked like the classified ad boxes that Rolling Stone magazine had back then. One of the boxes read "Vixen Battles: Sexy Female Wrestling. For catalogs, write to…" and it gave a P.O. Box in California. It would be another thing to have to watch out for in the mail. I guessed it would take about three weeks for my letter to get there and then for them to fill my order. My first idea with this was getting my hands on even racier videos, but it ended up being just enough, at least for then, to get material I could enjoy in my room without the high-wire act I was doing in the living room.

Plus, I wouldn't have to get any money to send in the mail. I knew where the stationery and stamps were in mom's desk drawers. I wrote on some paper, "Please send me Vixen Battles catalogs, here is my name and address." I only put the address on the envelope, not the name from the ad, in case anyone might see it in the mailbox waiting to go out. I hoped whatever arrived would be discreet on the outside.

Three weeks later, I'd again get antsy around the mail delivery time every day. Again I sat on the couch opposite the picture window, glancing out every time I sensed a vehicle passing by. On the third day of this routine, after about an hour, grandma came out and said, "There's mail for you." She handed me a standard size envelope that felt like it had a few sheets of paper folded up and crammed inside.

I took the envelope into my room, forgetting I had left the TV on, and shut the door. I opened it with a scissor from my little kids' desk, then laid down on my stomach on the bed. In very small type, the papers described different videotapes. There were several black and white pictures throughout. Matching the descriptions with the pictures, "Goldie" was a tan blonde in a black (or red) and white striped one-piece swimsuit. In one picture she posed in the center of a boxing ring. Another close-up picture showed her locked in a hold by a brunette girl, a grimace on her face.

Looking at this, I got hard again. I stared at that picture for a long time, then moved on to the other pictures and descriptions of the fight videos. I stayed hard and felt an electric buzz running through me. I kept going back to Goldie's picture, letting my excitement build until my dick felt swollen and sore. I looked away from the pictures, daydreaming about being in the ring with these girls. But I started to think about how impossible it would be for any of this to really happen. I didn't know what else to do beyond looking at the pictures, so the excitement subsided and I went back out to watch TV.

Power-Mad Fantasies

In real life, as a 14-year-old boy, I didn't know how to talk to girls. My only view about girls or women was this softcore porn I'd gotten. From that, I created a fantasy world in my head, dreaming of having power over women in a twisted fantasy. I would imagine grown women like I was seeing in the videos and brochures. At night, in bed, when I was supposed to be going to sleep for the night, I imagined having women in a dungeon under my house. In the fantasy, I'd pick a woman out of several in the dungeon to wrestle in a mud pit. I didn't know the mechanics of sex, so when that was done, I put her back in a cell, just like putting a toy back on a shelf.

On some level, I knew this was wrong, and I certainly knew this was something I would not actually do in real life when I got older. I never would have shared these thoughts with other guys I'd begun to befriend, because these thoughts seemed shameful. It wasn't until I grew up and heard about or read about real crimes against women, like abductions and worse, that I wondered if my dark teenage fantasies were the same as rapists and killers started out having. This made the memory of these thoughts even more shameful but also scary in a way. Still, I understood what was normal in real life enough to block the hormone-fueled insanity of being a teenager from spilling over into reality. I do think I needed the fantasy for the feeling of control it gave me, and as an outlet for sexual thoughts coupling with anger and frustration at my inability to get a girlfriend.

Meanwhile, back in the real world of 10th grade, I fumbled my reaction to a crush, putting a note in her locker rather than trying to speak to her directly about anything. Other boys my age at least knew how to get a date, and I envied that.

The Becky Story

In the junior year of high school, Becky sat in front of me in math class, often turning back to me and asking about the homework or whatever she didn't understand in Algebra II. We were in the front rows of the room, to the left after the teacher's desk. I'd sat there because I wanted to be able to still see the board without having to wear my glasses. I didn't like how I looked in glasses, or didn't want to seem like a nerd.

Becky dressed pretty preppy, often with a boys' style collared button down shirt. Sometimes with vertical red stripes – I remember that one distinctly. She was short, with a curly bobbed brown haircut that stopped short at the top of her neck. She had paler, whiter skin, on a circular face with brown eyes and eyebrows. The image of her turned in her chair to look back and talk to me, frozen in time, is stuck in my head all these years later. Her clean-cut, pretty look drew me to her.

31

The conversations were all like this – as we settled in waiting for the gruff lady math teacher to demand our attention, she'd turn around to me.

--Did you do the problems last night?

--Yeah.

--Can you tell me what was up with number 6? I don't understand it.

And I don't remember high school algebra or pre-calc all that well, but usually I'd have done that problem and gotten it right, so I'd then explain it.

--Thanks, she'd say.

And that would be the end of it—if she wasn't cut off by the teacher starting class before that exchange could be done.

All this time, all those little exchanges, it would be building in my head how much I liked her.

Finally, after months of this, I put all that longing into a little note asking if she'd go out with me. I couldn't find any chance where I'd get to be alone with her to ask her out, and trying to ask her in the middle of a crowded school hallway was too scary. I assumed all eyes would be on me, or at least they would be if anyone around realized what was going down. Getting rejected in front of others like that would have been humiliating and embarrassing.

So instead I resorted to a mild form of stalking. Coming and going from our class, or if I spotted her in the halls between classes, I'd keep an eye out or follow from a distance. That way, I found out which locker was hers, even checking the number of the locker after she was done, so I wouldn't get the wrong one for the note. That way I could find out if she liked me back without risking anything. Reconnaissance done, one day, I dropped the crumpled up little piece of ripped notebook paper into one of the slots in the top of her locker. If I knew she liked me back, then I'd be able to talk to her anywhere.

After that, there were a few days in class where I didn't know if she'd gotten the note at all yet.

But she wasn't turning around to talk to me anymore. I got that sinking feeling you get when something goes wrong, like no one calling back after a job interview, and you realize whatever you went after wasn't going to happen. The next day after that, I spotted an empty seat in one of the back rows of the room, and asked the kid next to it if anyone normally sat there. They said no, so I switched there without asking for the last several weeks left in the school year. I didn't want to be so close to Becky with that sinking feeling of failure.

At some point, someone relayed a message through the social circles to my best friend in school at the time, to tell me that Becky wasn't interested.

My grand plan, had Becky said yes to me, was to take her along to the big Genesis concert that summer. I just assumed she'd like the music I liked. It didn't matter that really I was the one getting to go with my friend Jason, his sister and their dad. I was dead set on commandeering a seat for my dream date. Talking to Jason, I set out to convince him that his sister was the weak link in who was getting to go to the show.

-I'm telling you, Becky's going to come with me to the concert. Why do you want to bring your little sister anyway? She's not into Genesis.

-My dad's taking us and he insists.

-Ah, this is how I'm going to impress her though, I have to do this.

There I was, browbeating Jason to let me have one of the tickets for the big concert at Vet Stadium in the summer, to bring a girlfriend I didn't actually have yet. My arrogance with my friend only dissipated once that relationship wasn't actually happening.

It was the 1987 Invisible Touch tour, when they had reached the height of their popularity. We had tickets for the cheapest seats in the stadium, about five rows from the absolute top of the concrete bowl, on the infamous "700" level. Veterans Stadium in Philadelphia was the all-purpose football, baseball and concert venue—utilitarian, almost Soviet if not for bright red, orange and yellow levels of seats and the bright green Astroturf field. It was all we knew as kids, never having been to any old classic ballparks in other cities, and before the retro ballparks to come in the 1990s.

Because I experienced the Vet in this way as a kid, going to Phillies games, it was still imprinted in my brain as a fun place. And when we did finally go to that concert, it was where I experienced one of the most powerful rock moments in my young life to that point. The track was "Unquiet Slumbers ... In That Quiet Earth," a bombastic instrumental from their 1977 album "Wind & Wuthering," an album I had not yet heard before the concert. "Unquiet Slumbers" has this moment where the blaring keyboards are playing a passage at top volume – and in concert, this was definitely top volume, reaching the cheap seats. Then there's a quick silent pause, punctuated with a few slashing guitar chords where the rest of the band is silent behind those. At full stadium concert volume, it was even far beyond what I can do today playing back the same track at top volume on modern equipment. That was the moment that blew my mind, and I had to find out where that piece of music came from.

It was at a time when Genesis was as popular as it ever was with the general public, but even then among rock music fans, they weren't seen as cool as late 70s punk rock or the forerunners of grunge in modern rock that were just starting to develop. I like a lot of that music, but it was in that unlikely stadium setting that Genesis cemented itself into my musical preferences for the long haul – something I'd always circle back to.

City Gardens

In the great modern classic movie "Almost Famous,"
there's a scene where Phillip Seymour Hoffman, playing
rock music writer Lester Bangs, tells the precocious
reporter kid, "I've seen you, and you are not cool."

That was me at that age, really into music and writing
about it, but definitely not cool. I wanted to work in the
hippest record store of the three in the local mall, and they
sneered at my (unwittingly) square appearance.

I wanted to hang with the cool kids who camped out
for concert tickets, and often went to the legendary local
punk club City Gardens, but only got invited along for
those nights a few times. Looking back I thought this was
just by virtue of proximity, not because I was particularly
cool. The leader of the pack for stuff like this was Seth,
who had been a classmate at the Hebrew day school I'd
gone to, but left for public school once that school moved

out of Trenton to Yardley, Pa., and got more expensive. I'd encountered him once again when I then went to public high school after being friends with him as a kid.

Seth seemed to have it all wired, being friends with seniors who could drive and get him in to that club. I definitely looked up to him as someone who was cool in all the ways I was not. He wore his punk rock and ska fandom confidently like a badge of honor, telling everyone about bands like The Toasters and 7 Seconds. I don't think I realized at the time that he had welcomed me into his circle and this world of music, caught up as I was in my own self-perceived unworthiness. I didn't claim to be into punk, but punk wasn't the only thing City Gardens had, also booking rock and later grunge acts that went on to much greater success.

One night I got to tag along with Seth and friends to see The Wailers, the late Bob Marley's backing band, at City Gardens. I'd become a big Marley fan, so I was excited. I'd heard about the reputation of the venue being a dangerous place. While excited, I also felt dread and fear as we pulled into the parking lot alongside the imposing concrete bunker of a building. The crowd of people entering and the stark parking lot lighting magnified the presence of the club in my memory of that brief moment in time. Here I was looking up at the legendary City Gardens, as we walked up. Maybe I was one of the crew, unlike how my inferiority complex made me see this later on, and just a little bit cool. I hoped we'd get in.

The way they talked, it wasn't a sure thing that we'd even get in, but we did. Inside, it was mostly black painted walls all around and a stage at one end. When we got in, there was already a crowd 20 rows deep. I tried getting on tiptoes to see over people's heads when the Wailers came on, but couldn't keep that up for very long. The crowd and atmosphere were scary, I wasn't used to what a club rock show could be like. The sound of the band was muddy and loud, not like listening to the clear originals at home, but I could feel the funky bass notes go through me. It's something I learned to love once I got to college and concerts like that basically came right to me on the campus, and I could go unfettered.

Much later in life, I'd read about and learn about how City Gardens looms large in the imaginations of punk and rock music fans, for all the great bands and artists who played there from the early 1980s through the early 1990s. I wished I recognized it at the time and went more often, especially since I liked a lot of those acts, but thanks to those classmates, at least I have that memory of one time there. Its reputation as a dangerous place may have had something to do with keeping me away from there, as timid as I could be about things.

*   *   *

There was another night around that same time, with Seth and two younger girls, Abby and Cindy, where we were camping out for INXS tickets. This didn't mean staying outside all night, but we had to be up for a while in Seth's den, so we could get a number for the line in the middle of the night. Then, closer to morning, come back to the mall where the ticket vendor was for the on-sale time. I guess this must have been a Friday night into a Saturday morning, because I don't know how I would have gotten to do this otherwise.

The friends were talking about Yellowman, a reggae singer, who'd either just played City Gardens, or was going to, and they were playing some of his music in the car. It didn't sound the same as Bob Marley. It was a lot closer to rap, with dirty lyrics rather than Rastafarian peace and love as its subject. To an unenlightened kid, this singer's bizarre appearance on the covers of cassettes seemed freakish. He is a Jamaican albino disfigured on one side of his face and mouth, which I had no idea then was due to cancer surgeries. To me, he just looked and also sounded scary and rough, but I stifled that reaction because I wanted to seem cool with everyone.

Going to City Gardens, hearing punk music, hanging out in the middle of the night, all put together, felt soaked in a dangerous vibe. I liked it more than I realized, because I would be drawn to it in college when it was easier for me to access. Those few outings and times did plant a seed and stick in my memory. Later in life, it turned out, Seth and I had a lot of the same values, and our families had more connections in the distant past than I realized.

Teen Scenes

I thought that after I graduated the Hebrew day school in eighth grade, that if I didn't get to go on to a private high school, I'd be disadvantaged. I feared public school too; that played into it. With perspective, though, I think my inferiority complex about my family's lack of money would have gotten worse if I continued to go to school with richer kids. At the tail end of my time in Hebrew school, there were a couple Bar Mitzvahs that were more extravagant and fancy, which made me feel out of place, even as an invited guest. There would have been more events like that had I stayed in private school.

So I went from being in small single-digit in number classes at the Hebrew school to a public high school with a few hundred kids at each grade level.

Just being quiet, shy and afraid of new interactions made me a target to be picked on in this new school environment. Even while trying to be noticed as little as possible, never dressing or acting in any way to call attention to myself.

One day on the bus home after school, I froze in my seat as I heard two Black kids behind me, talking about me, trying to provoke a response from me. I froze like a hunted animal and wouldn't respond. I didn't know what to do. Then they spit on the back of my head and neck. I stayed frozen. Their stop finally came, none too soon, and they got off the bus. I couldn't wait for my stop to come as I felt the spit running down the back of my neck. It was probably less than five minutes, but it felt like hours. I had to trudge to the front of the bus to get off, thinking everyone must be looking at me after seeing or hearing me get bullied.

This was different than being bullied on the bus to private Hebrew school, because that involved people somewhat like me, and I finally felt like I could tell somebody. Here, I didn't know what kind of people I was dealing with due to our differences, and I didn't feel like I could speak up to anyone.

Walking in the house, I hurried right to my mom's master bathroom, because it had a sprayer in the sink, took my shirt off and sprayed off the back of my neck and head. I never told anyone. It left that kind of a mark on me. I formed prejudices from this incident, I'm sure. I'd laugh a little harder at racial jokes. I'd shy away from black kids at school, at the mall or elsewhere -- cross to the other side of the street, so to speak. The diversity of college, and certainly out of adulthood, eventually made me more enlightened, but a remnant of that trauma still can surface sometimes. I'm sorry I didn't attempt to defend myself in the moment. I'm sorry for the scared kid I was.

Going into that new public school, the one link I had was Jason, who I'd befriended one of the summers before at the JCC. He was already in the school district, so he was one of only two people I knew when I started there. One classmate from the Hebrew school lived in the same town and did start 9th grade in the same school district.

With Jason, it was the first time I played out a pattern I would repeat many times as an adult. I'd befriend someone who was even nerdier than I was or even worse of a target for bullies than I was. I don't think I realized then that I might have done this so I could feel better about myself by comparison. We were close as young teens, staying over at each other's houses. Jason was a short guy, wore glasses and had awkward mannerisms and physicality. Much later as an adult, I'd befriend guys who resembled him, perhaps with even more extreme challenges in terms of awkward behaviors and appearance. One of those friends had Asperger's. I'm neurotic but I had the ability to shift into a social mode and pick up on cues. Still, I didn't acknowledge to myself that by doing this, I was making myself feel better about my own issues.

In keeping with that effort to be cool by comparison, when hanging out with Jason, I'd puff myself up. Jason would stay over and we'd camp out in sleeping bags in my living room. I'd bring out a few of my sports magazines' swimsuit girls issues. I'd open up one of the magazines, and point out a picture of Kathy Ireland that I liked, where she looked dusky, tan and Sphinx-like. Her thick eyebrows stood out in the picture, made her seem more exotic.

43

I acted like showing Jason these pictures was showing off my girlfriend and how hot she was. Except that wasn't my girlfriend and I was a long way from having one. Jason would react to my comments about the "hotness" of the women in the pictures with a high-pitched snickering, "yeah, yeah, yeah," sounding like Beavis from Beavis & Butthead. Each of us lay in those sleeping bags on the living room floor, looking at these magazines, unaware that the other one was probably pushing their boner into the floor.

White In The Woods

Ninth grade began for me at a public school in my town,
rather than the rarefied air of private Hebrew day school.
Being the quiet one, as I'd been in summer camp and
school before that, I got close to other kids from
proximity, rather than things in common. At the very
beginning of the year, I became friends with two working
class kids, John and Brett. John's house was a small, beaten
up, compact little place in a neighborhood just off a gritty
part of the township, a road that boasted a firehouse, a
hardware store and a neighborhood liquor store. John's
mom was around, and maybe an older brother. The house
had a stale cigarette smoke smell and dirty old carpeting.

I felt uncomfortable but these were my first friends so far,
or the first kids who'd befriended me. I didn't stay close to
them much beyond that year, but went on some adventures
before drifting away from them as the year progressed.

John was thin, wore an old dirty blue ski jacket, had a pockmarked face and short dirty blonde unkempt curly hair. Brett, already in 10th grade at the high school, had what looked like a beer belly and a 1950s' style square haircut.

The most vivid occasion I remember with them was a time when we rode our bikes exploring. John and Brett knew of some areas in the woods a bit north of us. One day after school, we rode over dusty ground, past bare trees, through fallen leaves, to a three-walled shack made of corrugated metal siding nailed to wood poles at its corners, with more siding thrown on top for a roof. The ground of the shack, also covered in leaves, had a few cinder blocks arranged in a circle, like some kids had sat gathered there before us.

-What is this, I asked.

-I heard about this place, Brett said, not explaining where or from who he heard about it.

-Cool, right? John said.

-It's a hangout, Brett continued. I bet they got some Playboys here.

-Yeah, John said.

Brett started kicking away the leaves, looking for those Playboys. He found a piece of cardboard he hoped was covering a stash in the ground, but it was an empty hole.

-Somebody must have gotten to this first, Brett exclaimed.

-Oh, I said, not knowing what else to say, as the wheels in my mind started to turn. If there had been magazines out there, I would have felt self-conscious looking at them in front of these other guys. I had kept that activity as private and secret as I could.

*   *   *

The only other incident I remember about these guys was
a time when John and I were waiting for the bus to take us
home from school, and it was taking some time, there was
some delay. The zipper on John's old ski jacket had broken,
and his coat was stuck shut. As I tried to pull it open for him
from the bottom of the jacket, above his crotch, some of the
other kids started mocking me as doing something gay. I
heard someone say "Look at him pulling on his zipper, ah
hah hah ha ha." Funny, but humiliating to me, with their
comments directed more at me than John, I thought.

The Big Man In Travel Camp

My town had a Jewish Community Center. It was an important place to me as a youth. My parents had met at a dance there. Their first attempts to teach me swimming as a kid took place there. Later, I went to day camp there, and then a teen travel camp that was centered there. Jason and I met there, in the teen rec room area. Still later, as an adult, I'd come back there when my family still had the membership and I'd swim laps in the pool there. Eventually, the JCC disbanded and the facilities were turned over to the town as a secular community center, and the pool became the town pool.

Between the Hebrew day school and high school, I went to the teen travel camp for two summers, around ages 13 and 14. The camp had day trips and a couple two or three night trips each year to the Poconos and Montreal, and even a weeklong trip to Southern California. When there wasn't a day trip, we'd go to the JCC's pool for the day. On those days, I'd bring my little boom box and a few tapes of music I liked. I wasn't picking music that I thought the girls would like, but I started to notice that some would gather and hang out because I had music. It gave me a little bit of a lift that I might be impressing them somehow.

On the mornings of those pool days, the school bus would pull up to the low-slung one-story tan brick building with about 15 of us teenagers on board. We'd file out into the plaza in front. Everyone would be in a happy mood, excited for a sunny day at the pool. Toting a little blue and white QT model Sharp tape player/radio, and cassettes in my bag, I'd anticipate seeing Marcy at the pool. She had thick dark eyebrows like Kathy Ireland in my magazines and wore an attractive one-piece swimsuit. Marcy had a mischievous smile and light brown permed curly hair that stopped above her shoulders.

Before us boys could get to the pool, we'd go into the bathroom to change. Its concrete block walls reach up to open air just under a wooden pagoda roof suspended on top. We all pick our little zones, spots along benches, to change into swim trunks, shy about being seen or inadvertently looking at each other while changing. Quick as possible, we rush out to the big grassy lawns around the pool.

I see Marcy and her friend Tabby already under the pavilion where they usually hang out. It's at the far corner down by the deep end of the giant L-shaped Olympic size-plus pool. I go striding down there, pull up a chair by them, say "hey" and pull out the boom box, start playing one of my tapes.

"What's that?" Marcy asks, pointing to the boom box.

"Peter Gabriel, Sledgehammer," I say.

That day I might have worn my Gabriel concert t-shirt from earlier in the summer. I point to it, exclaiming, "this is from his concert I went to." She smiles and I'm excited, feeling the full effects of my crush on her, but I can't think of what to say next. So I don't really hold her attention, but I get to be around her.

*   *   *

The camp's day trips and travel also brought me other brushes with the opposite sex. One day brought us to Point Pleasant Beach and its boardwalk, which had amusements and a small water ride park. The park had a water slide. You'd climb up three or four stories of stairs, carrying a thick but flexible mat to lie on to go down the slide. The slide tube had enclosed parts and other parts open to the sky on the twisting, turning way down. At the top, you stepped in an ankle-high pool frothing with a jet spraying a flow of water down the slide. You would lay out your mat, lay down on your back on it, and when the bored teenager manning the slide gave the OK, you'd push off.

That day, I fell in with a few other teens that weren't part of our group and we all ended up as a group together. One girl in the group stunned me with her looks and presence. She was more mature and also more magnetic than anyone else there. She wore a one-piece black-and-white striped swimsuit that showed a little cleavage, cut higher on her hips than most more modest girls of that age would do. She had straight dirty blonde hair down to her shoulders, and a round face with cute, small features.

51

Someone in the group got the idea to push off sooner than we each were supposed to so we could clog up the slide halfway down and bunch up in a tangle of legs and arms. Ending up next to this girl in the tangle thrilled me but I didn't want to freak her out if I got a boner that she would feel. So I tried to at least pull my crotch back from pushing right onto her. Still, our bodies were pressed together for a while, and this was incredibly exciting, even having to hold myself back.

Montreal Bus

During one of the teen travel multi-day tours, where we'd stay overnight at other JCCs, on our way up to Montreal, I became friends with a cute girl and we sat together on the bus. Other kids in the camp gossiped about her, saying she had her "tubes tied." That was very unlikely, I later realized. Maybe they were trying to put her down or socially isolate her, make her seem freakish to others.

I was prone to believing everything I heard, though. So if she tragically had her "tubes tied," that loomed large in my imagination. It made me like her more, if she might have a health problem. I could be her protector. This rumor made her more of a mystery to me.

I can't remember her name now. We only spent that one trip close together. It wasn't like we dated, so we didn't split up, just floated away from each other after the trip. While the time with her and also around Marcy never went anywhere for me at that age, I felt for the first times that I could be close to someone. That boosted my confidence, but in later years in high school, that all got slapped back when I asked out my math class crush.

The Big Men

Sometimes in summer camp and elsewhere, I gravitated to larger guys as friends. I thought this would protect me from bullying. I feared that more than most, even though no one in camp was bullying me. Outside of the Hebrew day school, the summer camp was wider exposure to other types of kids, even though it was still a Jewish camp.

On the Montreal trip, I remember I looked up to a counselor named Greg as being a cool dude. He had long curly rock and roller hair. Despite having a girl seatmate on the bus during that trip, I still remember feeling sad and friendless at Le Ronde amusement park. So I kept hanging around Greg, who must have been humoring me, letting me hang out with him, instead of pushing me off to go be around my fellow campers more.

This reminds me of another time during a school year before or after this, I'm not sure which, when I went on a

JCC weekend day trip to the Jersey shore. I didn't know anyone and wasn't fitting in. I sat by myself on the bus, moping and feeling sad. "Hello" by Lionel Richie played on a radio, magnifying my depressed, downtrodden feeling.

Why was I like this? My mom might have remembered better what was going on with me then. The abrupt change from the small Hebrew day school to the local public school left me alienated. I withdrew from everyone. It wouldn't be the first time. I'd do this again when I finished college early but turned into a loner lost in my college town. I'd do this yet another time as an adult in my 20s, when I also changed settings abruptly, moving from one town to another to pursue a journalism career.

But let's get back to my previous dysfunctional dynamic, sucking up to potential protectors. The travel camp had a different two-night trip to a rundown "ranch" somewhere in rural upstate New York. We stayed four to a cabin.

I was with Stu, a big guy I had befriended during the day trips in that session. There was another guy named Ira, who had a mop of curly Jew-fro hair and seemed to love talking crudely. None of us had any experience with girls, but Ira would boast about things he'd claimed to have done, like fingering a girl or spanking a girl. This was about as likely to happen as a teenage girl getting a tubal ligation. Ira thought his claims were entertaining and funny, but he seemed angry underneath. He tried to seem like a stud to us.

The ranch cabins looked like run-down motel rooms. Our cabin had worn, orange and brown bedspreads, fake wood-paneled walls and thick, beaten up and dirty dark brown carpet. Just one window let in light, with peeling white paint around its frame and threadbare orange patterned cloth shades on either side of it.

Later on, doing interviews with rock musicians, one once shared an off-the-record story about sex with groupies in the 1970s, and I immediately imagined it taking place in a room that looked like this.

Discovering the Underbelly

The JCC also had teen trips on weekends during the school year. One Saturday night, they took us out to an arcade hangout across the river in Morrisville, Pa., which had its seedy parts. While waiting to board the bus for the outing, I talked to a girl who wore a lot of black and denim, with jet black hair and pale skin—the gothic, hard rock look I sometimes liked. She smelled a little bit of stale cigarette smoke, but that made her more dangerous and appealing.

I thought we had some rapport going, even though I still wouldn't have known what to do with that. When we got to the arcade, the girl seemed to know a group of tough looking teens who were already hanging out there. In the days before cellphones, that seemed weird. She drifted away from me as soon as she saw them. I sat down with her again when we got back on the bus, but the connection was gone and I was afraid to ask about who her other friends were.

*   *   *

One friend from the Hebrew day school days ended up figuring in another one of these encounters with seedy elements or seedy behavior when I was a teenager. Originally I think the friendship split apart over him borrowing my sneakers at my Bar Mitzvah party at our house, without asking. Later, he turned up once on one of these JCC outings. I recognized him but stayed away.

There was always a big yellow school bus taking us teens out to wherever we were going. This time, it was a Phillies game. On our way back, he was sitting within earshot of me, with a girl. It was dark on the bus and I couldn't see what they were doing, but it sounded like they were making out, or maybe even putting hands under each other's clothes. I heard them whispering, and some moaning.

In "Close Enough," a story I wrote about this friend outside the focus of this book, sparked by learning of his passing a couple years ago, I didn't cover something of consequence that his mother said by the graveside, that feels relevant to the memory of this teenage night out. She said her son had taught her how tough it can be to be a boy growing up, especially when he got lost in something magnetic and exciting with girls. That's what I saw on that bus. And I'd seen seeds of that while we were in school together too.

In the Hebrew school, this friend and a couple other boys would talk about peeking up the skirts of the young religious teachers we had. These were orthodox Jewish women, like ones I'd later see in Central Park, who wore tight blouses and denim skirts high up their thighs. I was shy and afraid to try to join in their conversation. I knew it was disrespectful or creepy, the way they were talking. But that wasn't why I didn't try to join in. I just wasn't confident about girls, so the way they were talking intimidated me. Later as an adult I'd do worse stuff than anything they were being crude about, but I was still a good boy then.

The Amateur Stalker's Dilemma

There was a summer or two after I outgrew the teen travel camp, before I found my footing with a few friends in high school. I'd bike over to that same JCC pool. … One day it seemed to my amazement that I was carrying on a conversation with an attractive girl in a sexy swimsuit. I was very interested in seeing her again, but tried to accomplish this in my awkward stalking way, as I'd done other times.

Later that day, after I got home, I tried to find her in the phone book white pages, by her last name, which she'd told me. But there were too many listings for that last name. So I tried a few different numbers, starting with the ones I thought were in the town she said she was from.

When I found the right number for the right address, I got her dad, though. He was polite and took a message, but that was the end of that. This was a such a small and quick occurrence, but it felt significant as a connection I attempted all on my own, separate from school or friends.

Cruising Nerds

I'd had a few rock and roll nights, but a kid named Mark became the most regular and closest friendship in high school. Ties with him and a couple other mutual friends lasted into breaks from college after graduating, and even when I returned home to New Jersey after college, still looking for a job.

We'd drive aimlessly around our town. Mark and I would wind our way around different neighborhoods, from the poorer, grungier ones closer to Trenton, to the wide streets and big, mansion-like houses in the richer areas.

One better neighborhood, known as Delaware Rise, was down by the river between Jersey and Pennsylvania. It had fewer nighttime street lamps and you could see the stars better. It was a more peaceful atmosphere if you could afford it. Its two-story houses boasted large lawns, even some landscaping.

Mark had an encyclopedic knowledge of the addresses of girls we liked in high school. Some of this he gleaned from working the counter at the local pharmacy, where everyone's addresses would be on the prescriptions. So as we drove around, he'd point out, "that's Crissy's house," or "that's Barb's house." I'd come to learn the addresses, at least by site or location. I'd salute or comment when we'd pass the houses of ones I liked. A few of our favorites lived in Delaware Rise.

That neighborhood, and other nicer ones, connected from the side away from the river to the denser streets and neighborhoods. Those in turn bordered the older, poorer neighborhoods as you got closer to Trenton. As you drove along this progression from the rich homes by the river toward Trenton, more business areas and stores appeared. As you drove closer to Trenton, you'd see more cars parallel parked on the streets.

But beauty was beauty, and we didn't discriminate. There were stops on this sad tour in the middle and lower-class neighborhoods too.

The houses would go from simulated stone and brick in Delaware Rise to painted siding and maybe some brick in the middle of the town. As you neared Trenton, you'd see more aluminum siding, stucco or concrete, with smaller fronts to the houses.

As we'd drive, Mark might tell a story or two about one of his past girlfriends as we passed their house. He'd had two or three through high school.

The soundtrack for our drives was classic rock and modern rock radio. There was WMMR and WYSP from Philly. In the early '90s, after high school, when we did this, there was WDRE, a unique mix of classic rock, alternative rock, and new wave. It originated in Long Island, but suddenly got simulcast out of Philly, so we discovered it.

You'd try to keep the best music going, changing stations when they went to commercial or played something we didn't like. We created the night's experience, controlling the music, talking about the girls we remembered, even though they were all gone off to college.

*   *   *

Still doing these drives after being back in the town after college, we started out one night from Mark's neighborhood, close to Trenton. The drive begins with passing the house of another girl, not far from his, who I also had a crush on but never got bold enough to pursue.

-Alright, he says, you know this one is as out of your league as Becky, right? You're still not over that Valentine's note from ninth grade, are you?

-I think she did like me though, I say, deluded.

-She's been with some tough guy for five years already, he throws back at me.

Still I think about calling her, oblivious to how weird that would be.

We move on toward the riverfront of Trenton and Ewing, which has older houses than Delaware Rise, with a different style. Some have shaded porches, unlike other places in the town. Mark had an ex in this neighborhood too.

-Wonder what she's doing these days, I say as we pass her house, then pause for a minute. Do you actually know, I ask.

-She got a much older boyfriend. We still talk.

-What can you talk about after that, I ask, genuinely curious.

-Things stopped as friends, on friendly terms, so it's OK.

-I don't know how you do that, I say.

We continue north along the river and go into Delaware Rise, where we pass the house of another ex of Mark's. He slows the car. The house's lights are off. It seems like no one is home. He wonders if they're on a family vacation, or just the parents are. He wonders if she's out partying or away for the summer, but he doesn't know. This ex had a sexy edge to her. The other one was more of a girl-next-door type.

We move on to some of the girls I liked in Delaware Rise. There was one in particular here who I sat near in a science class and we talked about music. She liked New Order, so of course I bought their greatest hits album. I lent her a U2 tape and got afraid to ask for it back after a couple months. At the end of senior year, I fixated on having her sign my yearbook. During high school itself, I hadn't mentioned my interest in her to my buddies. Especially after we started pulling pranks by picking up realtors' for sale signs and lawn ornaments, and relocating them to other houses—and we dropped something on her lawn one night. I just hoped this wouldn't somehow get tracked back to me and my friends.

Back on our post college drive, we slow down passing her house and Mark asks, "hey, remember what we did here?"

Playing a little dumb at first, I say, "did we take something off the lawn?"

-No, he says, getting amused and enthused. Paul was picking up stuff from all over the place and dropping it here, for a few nights in a row. Mark laughs at the memory.

Ennui Leading to Idiocy

It all began that same year when I was new to public school after starting it off as friends with John and Brett. To Mark, I was "the kid that don't talk" in chemistry class. My first impression of him was he was the only other kid that liked Robert Palmer after the singer's part in the Power Station raised his profile.

The friendship began with Mark lending me tapes of Palmer's back catalog and then we got together outside of school. We had a couple short-lived attempts at starting a band, with Jason on keyboards, and Seth on lead guitar, jamming in my basement.

The thing to do back then was to take walks around our respective neighborhoods at night. We'd make a circuit around the grid streets of his neighborhood or the long loop of mine. Talking about funny ideas we'd thought of, TV and music. Sometimes, just sometimes

71

we'd get into more profound topics and personal history, like Mark's dad who was absent by choice.

Another friend or two got added to these walks and things got sillier, like a time when we went down a dark road to an overpass over I-95. There we posed in an odd formation when a car approached, bright headlights catching us in their beam. One of us had bent down at our knees, pointing off one way. Another one crouched down facing the opposite way, and yet another one faced another way, saluting to no one. The car stopped and the driver asked us if everything was OK. We didn't expect that reaction and we laughed at them after they left, like they were the idiot.

Once we all got cars, we'd chase each other around my neighborhood in a game we called "cat and mouse." My first car was a beat up 1979 Chevy Chevette, a tiny sub-compact, lightweight and cramped inside. One night I pulled into a stranger's driveway when the friend I was chasing had just used it for a K-turn to evade me. I started to do the same to change direction and the Chevette stalled out in their driveway. The homeowner's porch light came on and I freaked out. Frantic, I turned the key again with my foot hard on the gas pedal. The engine sparked to life again, and I peeled out, relieved.

This wouldn't be the last dumb or unsafe driving, either. Another time, I'd heard that a friend had to slam on the brakes when someone else in the car yelled out, "STOP SIGN!" It was the outlet from the neighborhood on to the main four-lane road. They would have barreled across and likely been t-boned by oncoming 50 mph traffic.

I still hung out with Mark and these friends for a

couple more summers during college, as a familiar and easy safe harbor, rather than exploring the world. We were all still under 21 but not sly enough to get fake IDs to go to bars or clubs. So we'd end up around someone's kitchen table playing marathon games of Risk at night.

The summer after junior year of college, I went to Los Angeles. The summer after senior year I still spent around campus in Maryland, trying to land a job in D.C. Then I returned to my hometown in New Jersey. I'd soon find out the changes that us all having turned 21 had wrought.

That first summer away in L.A. had made me something different. I'd grown up just a little sexually and mentally, but far from complete. But before that, there's all that happened at college, with new people, new encounters and new types of failings.

Freshman Dorm

At the very beginning of my first semester away at college in Maryland, my roommate and I met and started double dating two Asian girls who were roommates. Things fizzled between my roommate and the other girl, but he landed on his feet, meeting the girl he'd marry shortly after that.

Meanwhile, I kept hanging out with Jae. Her roommate had also moved on to a new boyfriend, and we all ended up in their room in the dorms one night. There was some nervous attempts to play strip card games, but I was still very shy and didn't want to take anything off. I lost my shirt but still covered up with a blanket, defeating the purpose of the game.

The time came that we all were ready to settle into bed. I got up on the top bunk bed with Jae, and the other couple was in the bed below us. I laid down next to her, under covers.

A week or so before there was a night where we all went bowling in the lanes under the student union. It turned out my roommate was out at his new girlfriend's dorm room, so I had the room to myself, and Jae came back with me. We sat down on my bed. I asked if we could kiss, and told Jae I'd never kissed anyone yet. She wasn't smiling. We were both very serious and awkward. We moved close and pressed our lips together, tentatively opening our lips just a little. We held it there in that moment for what felt like many minutes but was probably less than one minute.

After that, we stared at each other a bit. I wasn't feeling any romantic, loving draw to her, and it seemed like she wasn't in return either. Jae picked up her coat, put it on, and said, "I better get back." I nodded and led her out, no hug, no embrace.

But still, here we were, now in bed together. Maybe something would happen. I tossed and turned, and tried to get comfortable, first on my back, then on my stomach, and finally on my back again. Jae lay still next to me, on her back. She seemed to be already almost asleep. I looked up at the ceiling not too far above me, not knowing what to do, for what seemed like hours. I guessed we wouldn't kiss again, or anything else. Then my mind and my actions turned creepy, turned bad.

-I want to know what she feels like, a voice in my head said.

-Just go to sleep, or lay there and be quiet, answered my conscience.

-I think she's out, she won't know what I'm doing.

-Yes she will, or she might remember later.

-I don't care, I have to know what it's like.

With that, I slid a hand between the buttons of her pajama top. I felt around her breasts, running a finger around a nipple. Jae didn't stir. I ran my hand down her belly, toward her crotch, and down the front of her shorts. I felt some pubic hair, but got scared of going any further.

-Happy now?

-Is that all it is?

-Well, yes, said that wiser voice in my head, from the distant future. You'll see what will happen tomorrow.

-She probably didn't even feel what I did.

-It would have been impossible not to feel that, even half asleep. You'll see.

I rolled over, and tried to fall asleep. It took a long while.

We all started stirring as the sun came up through the window of the room. It was a Saturday morning, so there were no classes to get to. The good part of me knew I'd been a creep and should get out of there. Another part of me was in denial about what I'd done, so on Sunday night, I called Jae's room and her roommate answered. "She doesn't want to talk to you right now." I asked why, even though deep down I knew why. The roommate muttered something like, she's not feeling well.

I think I called her once, maybe twice more, still in denial about what I'd done. Eventually, I stopped denying it to myself and stopped calling. I never thought about acknowledging anything or trying to apologize.

Raelyn / Oh Fortuna!

She was a dark haired girl with tan skin that I met in one of the few science or math classes I took as a freshman in college. Her last name seemed Latina, but her look was punk rock – t-shirts and a dark green army jacket.

She'd befriended me, sort of, sometimes, as we'd sit there before class, waiting for the lecture hall to open. She'd sit next to me asking questions about the reading or my notes. I didn't think I knew the physics material that well but she had me pegged as a know-it-all nerd.

Raelyn would lean her leg against mine, just touching, maybe pressing ever so slightly. When she did that I felt a buzz rise up inside me but I would freeze, not knowing what to do about it. Even before she'd cozy up to me like this, I was attracted to her, but gun shy after the incidents with Jae the month before. I didn't know how to make a move back, maybe put my hand on her knee. I'd just freeze, stimulated by the moment but scared of reacting outwardly.

All I could do in those fleeting moments, was cry out in my head an exclamation "Oh Fortuna!" like Ignatius in a reverie in "Confederacy of Dunces" – as in, "woe is me, what am I to do? She is so exciting touching me but I don't know what to do!"

Dr. G

It's January 1990. I've returned to the office of the local
Jewish Family Service counseling center in my hometown.
It takes up a corner of a nursing home building, and has
its own entrance with a single glass door. I step inside the
familiar waiting room, seeing the receptionist's window
on the right. On the left is the door Dr. G would open to
bring patients in.

My mother brought my sister and I there for family
therapy with Dr. G, sometimes together, sometimes apart,
as younger teens. That started a love-hate relationship
with therapy at a young age. I vacillated between feeling
like I was being dragged to it and, later in life, needing it
and reaching out for it.

I was still 17, back home after my first semester
away at college in Maryland. Why was I doing this? I had
a 2.8 GPA in my first semester, but that seemed too low

and that upset me. I thought this was not up to snuff and worried that I wasn't going to succeed with college.

Now it seems like this was a silly thing to have worried about, but my anxiety wasn't diagnosed. Even just a couple years later, it then seemed silly. I'd improved my grades and that turned out to be the lowest grades I ever got. But at that time, it was the big looming monster in my world – all I could think about.

Dr. G emerged and showed me in to his office, with that wry smile on his face that he always seemed to have. He looked like Dustin Hoffman, with similar longer hair, like Hoffman had in "Kramer Vs. Kramer."

--So, Michael, why are you here?

--I'm worried about school.

--You went away to college, right?

--Yeah, I did. University of Maryland.

--Good school, good school … So, how was your first semester there?

--Well, I did have fun. But my grades weren't too good.

--What's 'not too good'?

--A 2.8.

Dr. G pauses for a few seconds and says:

--You know, that really isn't that bad.

--It's bad, I reply.

--That's not flunking out.

--Yeah, but it's not good.

He pauses again.

"You know, it's hard to adjust to leaving home the first time," he says, letting that idea hang in the air, in silence, for a moment. "It was a new situation for you. Let me ask you, what was fun about it?"

--I joined the student union group. We put on movies, concerts, events, I said, the pride filling my voice and showing in my posture.

--That's good. Did you spend a lot of time on that?

--I don't know, I shrug. I didn't feel like I did.

--Maybe you should do a little less of that when you go back, he suggests. You don't have to cut it out entirely. Anyway, I do think your grades will get better once you're more used to being there. And a 2.8 is really not so bad that you should worry about it. You're gonna be okay.

I wasn't convinced. I wondered if I spent more time on activities than classes, but recalled reading and studying most weeknights. I should study on weekends too. I should study as much as I can get away with during my campus job.

It's so hard to be patient, I thought. I agonized about having to get through another set of classes to get better results -- if I did. But there was nothing I could do about it. I thanked Dr. G, shook hands and left.

Why I Don't Really Like Pink Floyd

In college, midnight movies called out to me with promises of transgressive sights. Bad taste, sexual actions, freaky visions. It's where I first got exposed to Russ Meyer movies, the crazy surrealism of Jodorowsky, "Heavy Metal," and more. But among all those midnight movies, one in particular was my white whale. I could never get into it and never liked it. That was "Pink Floyd's The Wall." It also fucked with my head.

To this day, I usually change stations if a Pink Floyd song comes on the radio, except for maybe "Another Brick In the Wall," even though that's from this movie. There's a doom and gloom to songs like "In The Flesh," and many other "Wall" tracks, that's just in a different vein even than gloomy stuff I do like, like The Cure. Even Pink Floyd songs that aren't on that album or movie just turn me off, because they're similar. I've got to change the station.

Every time our campus theater showed "The Wall," it seemed like I was in a deep funk about a girl I was interested in or had an obsessive crush on. If not that, then a general self-hating depressive funk. Scenes in this movie showing the main guy going crazy and being straitjacketed in a padded room, would metastasize my bad mood. The booming soundtrack and the marching fascist armies on the screen amplified the doom and gloom I felt about romantic failures. I'd sit through the whole movie even as it made me feel more like shit, out of some twisted notion of giving art a fair chance, or a compulsion to finish whatever I started watching. It never occurred to me that it's OK to walk out of a movie!

So after the "Wall" finished around 2:30 in the morning, I'd trudge, tired, across the dark campus, back to my dorm, defeated and alone.

The Cry-For-Help Note

I'd achieved something being part of the student union activities group, winning a vote to be head of the movies committee for junior year. I took it seriously, but I took it too seriously. By the second half of the school year, I started to feel like I wasn't doing a good job, because I wasn't doing as well as the chair from the year before at getting the committee to bond and do stuff together. I beat myself up for not being as good socially.

In a state of overthinking this, I wrote this long letter to fellow leaders of the different activity groups in the student union council, complaining about what I felt I wasn't doing well. Ran off copies of this pathetic, self-flagellating letter and put them in everyone's box in the student union council office.

The concerts committee chair did express concern, but even though I'd written this, I wasn't receptive. Maybe

I wanted to complain more than I wanted actual help. She said, basically, don't take it so hard, and then expressed something about watching out for warning signs of suicide. Even though I reached out, I then felt and acted offended, because deep down that wasn't the attention or help I wanted. I think I just wanted someone to wave a magic wand and make me better socially, and then I'd feel and seem more successful in that role. It was all meant to be a fun volunteer experience but I took it very seriously.

Los Angeles

Eastern part of Santa Monica, about a mile west of Century City, Southern California, summer 1992.

I sit on a twin bed in the spare bedroom of a modest apartment. It's nighttime. I shut the light in the room, sit on the floor and peek up and out the bottom of the window. I'd spotted the outline of a young woman in a window of a building across the street. I wished for binoculars.

The next day is a Saturday. It's mid-afternoon. My aunt and uncle who I was staying with there had gone out to their house in the suburbs. I'm sitting on that same twin bed. I pick up the issue of the L.A. Weekly off the pile of books and magazines on the nightstand. I flip to the back pages with the ads for massages. With a pencil, I make little marks next to ads I think have the right code words, like "sensual" or "full body." Or ads that describe a masseuse so I can picture her in my head, with words like "discreet young brunette" or "Swedish blonde."

I go into the eat-in kitchen, bring the cordless phone back to the room, and call one of the numbers. Answering machine. I hang up. I try another number, one of about two or three I picked out. I was well into college at this point, and I'd given up on trying to get close to any girl with just my own wits or personality.

Another answering machine. I hope, if I leave a message, that they'll call back today, not after my aunt and uncle get back during the week. I say, "I'm calling about the ad for a massage. I'd like to get a massage," and then I hear a young woman's voice say "hello?"

I ask, "What is the massage like? I mean, is there something extra that you do?" The woman says, "Well, it's $75 for one hour, and you also can tip."

"Where do I go to?"

"I'll have someone call you back with the address. Around what time?"

"7 o'clock?" I ask, planning to eat dinner before going.

*   *   *

A few hours later, I have an address in hand that I looked up on my local map. It must be up in the hills north of Westwood. I go catch the local "Big Blue Bus," at a stop up on Santa Monica Boulevard. I take a route that goes up through Westwood, past UCLA, then to a wooded area along Sunset with little activity or buildings around to be seen. Right there, I press the stop button and get off at a bus shelter carved out of the edge of the woods. I walk a couple minutes up to the road to an intersection without crosswalks. I cross Sunset and start walking the shoulder of a road that is winding uphill.

Every few minutes, cars zip by on the road, very close to me. I hug the bushes at right, walking on the narrow shoulder. If I looked up I might see the houses up in the hills beyond the woods or bushes, but I have to keep my eyes forward. When no cars are passing, I veer left so I don't have to stay so close to the wall of green.

It seems like hours, until I finally start seeing address numbers along fences or on mailboxes. There are hundreds of numbers to pass, but they go up more than just two at a time, so it's about 20 or 25 properties that I walk past. I find the address she gave, in iron letters on a gate in a white fence with no gaps to see through.

I feel a lump in my throat from excitement. I brace myself to push the button on the speaker box attached to the locked gate. A woman's voice comes through the speaker with a lot of static, asking who it is. I give my name and mumble something about a massage appointment, wondering if they can hear me. Then I hear the woman say, "Just a minute." My anticipation builds. Then I hear steps from behind the gate, some fumbling with the lock, and the gate opens.

I see a tan young woman – older than me, but in her 20s – dressed in jean shorts, a satin slip top covered with a lacy vest, with the straps of the slip slung over black bra straps that lead down to modest but sexy cleavage. Her long dark brown hair is teased up and out in a very rock-and-roll, Sunset Strip rocker chick style. "I'm Michelle," she says. I'm nervous, but excited, wanting something to happen.

She takes me by the hand, leads me down a little sidewalk path to a small guest house a few yards in. I'm focused on her and where we're going, but a glance down the path reveals a larger main house further along. The girl opens the door of the little guest house, more like a freestanding guest room. The light is dim, and there's thick brown carpet in the front half of the room, and tile in the back, around a massage table. There's clutter around all the walls of the room.

"What would you like this evening," she says.

"A massage," I say, shy and low. "What we talked about, the price is $75?"

"Okay. For $100, you can have something a little more."

"What would that be?"

"Release."

I can guess what that means, but don't completely know for sure. It sounds good though. I don't think it's sex for that amount of money, but it's probably something. Maybe she'll let me touch her.

She tells me to get comfortable on the table. I strip down to my briefs, pick up a towel from the table, lay face down and put the towel over my back and legs.

She rolls the towel down to my butt and puts oil on my back. She starts pressing into my shoulder blades and lower back. I fixate on how close she is to me, with her waist right at eye level. Out of the corner of my eye, I see her very tan inner thigh as she touches me. I start to get hard and I'm pressing it into the table.

Michelle has me turn over now, and I'm aroused under the towel. She gets close, massaging my shoulders and then down my arms. While she stands close to the table to do this, I put my hand on her inner thigh. She doesn't slap my hand away, lets me keep it there, but I feel a vibe that if my move my hand anywhere else on her, she will.

"Do you still want we talked about?" she asks.

"Yes."

"Okay, so you can give me a tip for that now."

I sit up from the table, reach into the pocket of my pants on the stool next to it, and hand her the extra cash.

"Thank you," she says. "Now, where were we?" She guides me back down to the table, on my back, and begins rubbing up my legs. I'm feeling every move she makes. I see that she took off her vest and top and is just in a bra now, and I stare at her breasts, not what she's doing with her hands. Before I realize it, she takes the towel off and has her hand on my dick. She wraps her hand around it. The most intense stimulation I've ever felt whips through me, levels beyond when I was a kid wrapping a blanket around my crotch or just getting excited by the Sports Illustrated swimsuit issue.

Then she starts gripping my hard dick, tightening her hand around it and starting to pump her hand up and down on it. I'm overcome by pleasure running through me till I can't focus my gaze anywhere and just look straight up at the ceiling. Control gone, I feel her hand pumping as the sensation builds and builds, then abruptly releases. "What's happened?" I think. My eyes focus again and I see that I came. I'd had wet dreams, knew what cum was, and how it happens, but never felt that before. I see the stuff all over my belly, and then notice that Michelle has stepped away from the table.

She comes back with a wet washcloth and lays it on my belly. "Clean yourself up and whenever you're ready, you can get dressed," she says.

Hyattsville House

In the last year of college, the house I shared with roommates sat on a corner in a neighborhood where the numbered streets tangled around each other. 40th Avenue intersected 40th Street, and then intersected a different numbered street elsewhere after looping around the block. This was confusing if you didn't live there. The houses all looked small on the outside and sat close together to each other. Most were partly red brick in front. The house had two floors, but you couldn't tell from the outside, except for two windows jutting out of the slanted roof.

Stepping inside, wall-to-wall grubby brown carpet covered a big main room. To the right, we had a dining room table. I kept a stack of eight or nine Washington Posts on one end of it, and my roommates had odds and ends over the rest of it. On the left wall, toward the back of the room, a 20-inch TV sat on a beat up set of wooden shelves, with a VCR on one of those shelves.

95

Turning left at the front of the main room was the kitchen, where piles of dirty dishes would sit, all the way up to the top of a deep sink. A set of stairs behind the refrigerator led up to three bedrooms and a bathroom on the second floor. Going up the stairs, mine was the one on the right that had windows overlooking the front of the house.

I graduated early, but still finished out the school year living in this house, while looking for work in D.C. This wasn't good for me mentally. I'd convinced the inter-departmental copy center where I worked part-time on the campus to increase my hours to full time. But I wasn't a student anymore, so I couldn't continue with the student activities groups I enjoyed. So that isolated me. It didn't occur to me to reach out or do something socially to fill that void for my mental health.

Just six months after my time in L.A. being friendless and isolated, I was in the same boat, and that kind of situation would strain my mental health. I'd stopped getting along with my roommates in the house, which worsened my isolation. I would burrow inside my own head. I fixated on finding magazines with pictures of women for jerking off, having learned how to do it from the massage girls in L.A. Even this took some effort, because there wasn't yet Maxim or Stuff each month, and I didn't want to buy porn in person.

One night I remember coming back to the house after creeping around a local convenience store looking for magazines. I was back to being my 14-year-old self at my hometown Quick Chek, trying to be invisible while looking for what I wanted. I brought home a GQ that had a picture of an actor with a few sexy women (in swimsuits) vamping around him. In my room, lying in bed, gazing at the pictures, I get worked up and start pressing my erection into the bed. Then something stopped me.

I could hear a couple of my roommates, who I hadn't been getting along with, whispering outside my door. "I think he's masturbating again," one said. The other replied, "He's doing that all the time. He's such a fucked-up creep." I could hear them and it stopped me mid-stroke, but it wasn't as bad as being Alex in "Portnoy's Complaint," with mom knocking on your door, yelling, "what are you doing in there?"

Once the spring semester ended, I was still on the lease through the end of the summer, and I had the campus job, so I stayed there. The roommates all left and sub-let their rooms. Then I got a paid communications internship in D.C. for the summer, but I realized once that ended, I'd move back to New Jersey, since nothing else was happening for me.

In the mental state I was in, I didn't reach out to the new roommates either. I don't remember their names all these years later, after only being in the house with them for about three months. But I took the opportunity to move to a bigger and better room on the first floor. A couple moved into the other first floor bedroom. Their vibe wasn't exactly "hippie," but definitely on the Vermont "granola" spectrum. I haven't remembered their names. The guy was big and heavy set and his girlfriend was also a little heavier, and also busty.

I wondered about her, daydreamed about her sexually, maybe even pictured her while masturbating. Later, once I had a real job, if I liked a girl in the office,

I'd picture her just like that. Anyway, at times I'd be in the house alone and everyone else would be out. So I'd creep into the couple's room and look at her bras in their dresser drawers. I didn't go beyond that, but I definitely got a charge out of doing that. I was more of a bra guy than a "panty sniffer."

Avoidant Personality

For about five months after graduation, I'd hovered around campus, trying to get my life started. That doesn't seem like a long time now but it's a much greater percentage of the life of a 21-year-old. Depression was getting to me and I didn't even know that's what it was. So I went to a psychiatrist just off-campus, whose office was in a plain, anonymous, tan one-story building.

The psychiatrist was a short, thin, balding, bespectacled middle-aged, Jewish man. He seemed meek, but like he might be very smart. He asked about my situation and circumstances. I told him I worked on campus even though I'd graduated.

--What do you like to do when you have free time? It sounds like you have a lot of free time now. Do you see friends?

--Not really, I shrugged. I'm kind of on my own right now. I'll go to movies, maybe go into D.C. for the smarter movies. I can't go around the Hoff anymore since I'm graduated.

--Do you see any of your college friends?

--Not really. I'm in a house with roommates but I don't get along with them. I don't talk to them or hang out with them like I used to.

--Why not, the doctor asked.

He started checking some boxes on a prepared worksheet, but the print was too small for me to see the details of it. Each line had numbers preceding a few words, likely diagnostic codes.

--I don't like the roommates. We had been friends, but they don't keep anything clean, and I can't get them to do it. Now they leave me out of whatever things they're doing.

With his pencil, the psychiatrist tapped a few of the codes on the worksheet, and said, "It seems like you have an avoidant personality disorder."

I couldn't respond, but I did think, "That's a disorder? There's something wrong with me?" Today, it still sounds like such a damning assessment of a person, but also just a description of someone refusing to try to get out of their own shell, not necessarily a psychiatric disorder.

--What should I do with this, I asked.

--You could come back and see me again, but first you should start talking with a therapist. There's no medication I can prescribe.

At least in 1993 there maybe wasn't as much that could be prescribed, and talk therapy wasn't as mainstream as it's become. Other than that, I didn't even know enough then to ask for help finding a therapist, or a recommendation. This psychiatrist was cold and blunt.

His head was in the paperwork. Feeling lost and numb, I paid the fee, asked if I could get a referral and trudged out of the office. I didn't end up with a referral or a therapist, or didn't follow up at that time.

This psychiatrist caught me right when avoidant personality disorder first develops – early adulthood. I've read that this disorder keeps people from pursuing work or educational opportunities, but it seems like the reverse was happening. Being out of the loop of school or a career-track job caused my avoidant behavior. At that time, the labeling of this as a disorder was less than 15 years old, having first appeared in the DSM in 1980. The psychiatric profession didn't grasp the dimensions of this "disorder" yet.

That phrase, "avoidant personality," stuck in my head for a very long time. For years, I'd feel inferior and uncomfortable in social situations because of this "avoidant personality."

Nightclubbing

That visit to the psychiatrist was toward the tail end of my time in Maryland, just before I officially gave up on finding work in D.C. and moved back to New Jersey. Once I returned, I went back to spending time with those high school friends, who hadn't really left the area either. But now we were all 21 and could get into bars and clubs without needing fake IDs.

A typical Friday night would start around 9 p.m. Mark and I would convene at Adam's house because it was closest to the bridge into Pennsylvania. Before we'd hit the road, we'd sit in his den, and shoot the shit with his dad. Every time, as we headed out for our night, Adam's dad would laugh, "Here you are just starting your night, and I'm ending mine."

"That's right," we'd say, proud of ourselves, never thinking the day would come when we'd be winding down at this time of night.

Once it rolled around to 10 p.m., and we realized the time, we'd get it together to leave. We took turns being the sober driver these nights. In the winter, we'd leave wearing ski jackets, but when we got to the club, called "The Fizz," at a suburban Sheraton in Langhorne, we'd leave the coats in the car. This was out of a combination of thinking we'd look cooler without the coats on and not wanting to pay to check coats. We'd also go to other places past Langhorne or all the way to Philly's Delaware Avenue waterfront. It seemed like the most exciting thing going on in our world in the mid-'90s.

You'd enter the brightly-lit Sheraton lobby, go off to the right toward a glass door with darkness behind it. Stepping inside, a bouncer would check your ID. Then you'd be in a dark and loud space, with '90s club music booming and blaring. Not the big-city house music of the time, but radio hits like "Rhythm of the Night," "What Is Love" (think SNL's Roxbury Guys), "I Like To Move It," and "This Is Your Night."

The Fizz wasn't that big, but seemed vast at first, with a giant wrap-around bar, then another room past the bar. Off to the other side, a couple steps led down to yet another room with a dance floor. The ceilings were low for a nightclub. Streams of fluorescent light cut through the darkness in these rooms. The air felt cold and thin – like the oxygen-deprived air in a casino. Here the idea was to cloud your judgment into buying more drinks.

The more we went, the more we got a sense of spots to stand in and hang out, staring at girls among the crowd. Adam was the most relaxed and best at approaching girls there. Most of the time, I wouldn't have been able to tell you why I was even joining them in going there. I must have thought I would meet a girl at these clubs, but we'd get there, and I'd freeze. I wore louder shirts and dressy pants that made me look like the life of the party, but my demeanor negated that.

I'd take gulps from the first bottled light beer of the night, reaching the bottom in what seemed like just a few minutes. I'd push my way back to the bar, then go slower through a second bottle, and usually later a third one. I'd fidget, sway from side to side, not committing to dancing to the music. I'd grip my beer bottle, pick at its label, peel the edges off.

By the third bottle, the cheap beer didn't taste like anything, not like craft beers later would. I'd feel drunk and addled, which shed some of my discomfort and awkwardness. But I wasn't getting any sparks going with any girls, so I'd give up on that and get bored being there. I'd start to wonder when my friends would finally want to leave. I'd hope we weren't going to stay all the way to closing time, which was 1 or 2 a.m., but we often did.

The After Party

After closing time, we'd go to diners to eat. We'd often double all the way back into Jersey, 15 or 20 minutes drive beyond Adam's house, to go to our favorite diner. This I enjoyed more, freed from social failure in the club, instead able to see my friends and talk. This is where the jokes and banter would fly. My go-to order was a toasted bagel with cream cheese and jelly, with coffee. The waitresses hated us for our cheap orders. These nights in the diner inspired me back then to write a short story with dialogue that fell short of its Tarantino aspirations.

That all changed when my friends found a trio of young nannies from England and Germany, in the U.S. on work visas, who were also regulars at the Fizz. It was a natural and easier way to hook up because a social vibe sprung up. Nannies from their exchange program all knew each other. So we'd meet other ones, even ones who just arrived to the U.S. and our area.

The "after party" soon shifted from the diner to one or another of the host families' houses. The nannies kept drinking after the club, especially if their host family was on vacation. My friends had more "game" with the girls. They weren't aloof like me. Just like at the clubs, at these girls' houses, I'd stay in my shell and feel inferior.

I also had a misguided sense of honor. I'd choose who I wanted to pursue from the nanny group only after it was clear who my friends had picked. They seemed to figure out who was more attainable, too. I'd be left with whoever was the most wild, alcoholic and dysfunctional -- of course the worst match for my shy, conservative, square personality.

There was a short busty brunette named Oona. One night we were back at one of their houses, with the lights all low, and we decided to crash there till morning. I ended up next to Oona, on the floor, with our backs against the lower part of a couch, nodding off. She leaned on my shoulder. I had learned a lesson from being frozen out at the beginning of college by the girl I'd touched while she slept. Next to Oona, I wanted to do something again, but restrained myself, not out of respect but a fear of consequences. If I did something creepy, my friends would find out. I'd be shamed and embarrassed. Other guys might not have restrained themselves. If she was in this situation a lot, some guys probably did take advantage of her. Other guys might have had friends who wouldn't shame them for it, either.

So I could feel the warmth of Oona against me and that felt exciting, but I had no idea of what to say when daylight came. Before then, she got up at some point and laid down on the couch, and I went to another couch to sleep.

Another time out with the nannies, I got a better idea of the full dimensions of this girl's wild behavior. "Maui," on Delaware Ave., had a Hawaiian beach theme complete with sand volleyball courts. There one night, Oona binge drank until she ended up in the outside part of the club, sitting on a curb, throwing up. So I understood that this girl wasn't for me. This took some of the sting out of not hooking up with her. I saw this happen and didn't help her. I didn't know what it was to care for someone, to step in and hold their hair back.

More About Maui

The indoor part of "Maui" was a cavernous barn, with rear exits to an outdoor pier over the river. The outside area had another giant bar, the beach volleyball, and lots of space to drink, dance and party.

The indoor part could hold hundreds of people. A giant dance floor dominated one side, with steps up to another space where you could stare down at the people on that floor. On the other side, there were more spaces separated by rails and levels a step or two up or down. You could see around the whole interior.

By midnight or 1 am on a busy night, the place would get packed like general admission at a rock concert. You'd have to push through the crowd to get to one area or another, or to the bathrooms back by the entrance. You'd always end up somewhere else in the club and have to work your way back to go piss.

As at most nightclubs, bright pointed beams of light punctuated Maui's dark interior. The lights were combinations of purple, red, blue, orange and green. The music blasted from concert amp size speakers throughout the club. They played pulsing club music, but they would also throw in current rock and pop hits. I remember them sometimes playing rockier stuff, like "Creep" by Radiohead.

One night, in that packed crowd, I'd had drink after drink. There was nothing else to do. I never felt like I should go out on the dance floor by myself. On the nights, I'd taken to splitting off from my friends, planting myself at spots around the club and watching the girls in the crowds and on the dance floors. I knew I was drunk as I found myself pushing through a crowd to go elsewhere in the club for no real reason. The crowding was my excuse to grind myself into girls in front of me. One turned her back, disgusted, while another pushed forward to get away from me. Before getting those reactions, I was enjoying doing this. I was drunk and getting off on it. I should have been thrown out or worse, but in that crowd I got away with it.

In those moments, I was pretty far gone, on my fourth drink or more, which was a lot for me even then. Somehow I never blacked out from drinking, only because I was an intense control freak.

Even being there with friends, and being around so many people, I was still very alone in that place.

Studio 27

I found out from my friends about another place, and would go there on my own. New Jersey used to have many go-go bars, the lower-rent old-school version of giant "gentleman's club" strip clubs. Go-go bars were dives that would have a wraparound bar with a stage for strippers behind it. There was one down the road from Princeton, about a 30 minute drive from the house I grew up in and returned to after college.

I'd drive down Princeton's Nassau Street, then continue as it became dark and woodsy Route 27, through Kingston and onward. After Kingston, the road got dark, then lit up a bit with sporadic shopping plazas and little businesses. The drive seemed longer than it was from all my anticipation about where I was heading. The destination was a strip shopping center with a florescent-lit lot, empty except for a cluster of cars by one storefront, the Studio 27 go-go bar. Every time I arrived there, waves of excitement went through me, as I got out of my car to walk in.

Opening the dark door to the go-go bar and entering to see girls dancing on the poles was always an intense moment. I'd go sit wherever I could that had empty seats on either side of mine. I'd pace myself with the drinks, because I didn't have any friend with me as designated driver. I'd nurse marked-up cheap beer for hours, usually having no more than two. The speakers blared heavy metal and hard rock – like Guns N Roses, Motley Crue, also Rage Against The Machine – creating an aggressive vibe. Guys tipped the strippers with dollar bills. The girls let them stick the bills in the sides of their g-strings or between their breasts. You could cop a feel as you slid in a dollar.

I would spend two drinks or two hours there, and then leave to drive back home with a plan. I'd nurse a hard-on the whole drive back, back through Kingston and Princeton, onto I-95 for a few exits to home. I'd arrive back home with a throbbing dick. I'd rush upstairs to my bedroom to jerk off to mental pictures of the strippers, hours after my mom and stepdad had gone to bed.

I developed this nursed-boner routine until I could do it all the way back from bigger strip clubs near Philly. If I said where I was going at all, I likely said I was going out with friends and being social.

Super Bowl of Humiliation

The culmination of all this came about two years later, around the time of the 1996 Super Bowl. The circle of hometown friends had grown, adding other high school classmates and friends we'd made at college. Some were all living together in an apartment and a house. In the past couple years, there had been spring break trips to Florida, and I wanted to get to go with them on the next one.

They planned to go on their next Florida trip without me knowing, thinking I wouldn't find out. Of course, one guy in the gang who they supposedly didn't like but tolerated anyway, started blabbing about it in front of me at our Super Bowl party. It took a minute to sink in, but when I realized what was happening, I started stewing.

I blocked out any memory of the rest of the party, consumed by being cut out of the fun trip I'd wanted to go on. I don't remember even watching the game. I don't think I stayed for it. I left the party not long after the game started. On the way out, as I walked off, I thought I heard one of the guys berating the blabber for blowing the secret.

What bothered me most was that Mark, who I thought was my close friend in the bunch, never spoke up for me. For a couple months or more, I didn't speak to him, much less anyone else in the group. I'd invested too much in that friendship.

As I sealed myself off from contact, I got more lonely. I had a job and colleagues, but no more friends to hang out with outside of work, even as dull as the nightclubbing got for me.

It came to a head one morning in April at Princeton Junction train station, planning to go to New York to see "Late Night With Conan O'Brien" in person. I had been excited for this day.

I sat in my car in the crowded parking lot where I was lucky to find a space, thinking, going back and forth yet again in my head.

--I really want to go see this, I thought as I read over and over the letter from NBC that served as an audience pass. Maybe it will make me feel better.

--But why am I doing this by myself? I should be doing this with a friend. Why bother?

Beating myself up.

--What does it matter whether I go see this show or not? I still don't have anyone or anything going for me.

I start to well up and cry, putting my head down on the steering wheel, thinking.

--I don't even feel up to doing this anymore. I'm not going to enjoy it.

116

The devil won out.

I punched and slammed the steering wheel a few times, angry and also crying. I never got out of the car to go buy a train ticket.

I looked up and out of the windshield again at the field of cars parked in front of mine. I was dazed in the way you might be after you're all cried out about something. I've decided I'm not going. I dig out a tissue and dry my eyes. I turn the key and back out of the spot to head back home.

That night I call Mark for the first time in months and end up meeting him for dinner.

The Story of V

After a few months in my first job for the newspaper group, a young woman joined as a reporter on the staff. The reporters there were mostly guys, except one other woman there. She was in the same age range, early 20s, but carried herself with maturity light years ahead of us, and wouldn't go near any of the guys socially.

But the new hire seemed obtainable. We sat in rows of two side-by-side desks each – about five or six rows from the front of the newsroom to the back. The new hire, V, took the desk to my right in one of the middle rows. She was short, petite, with a mousy, nerdy but sexy librarian appearance.

I got a strong crush on her, like my first high school crush. A few years older now, after my L.A. experience, I'd fantasize about her sexually. My fantasies were passive. I didn't know what she'd do to me, but I pictured her in my head sometimes while masturbating. Not even creating an undressed image of her, but channeling all the emotion of my crush on her into a sexual feeling.

Another reporter there, Tom, was also interested in her. I didn't like him much even before that, because I found him obnoxious. But that sealed my dislike of him.

V and I did hang out a few times in the months after she started. Maybe those counted as dates, but she probably didn't think so. The newspaper office was halfway between our hometowns. We both were living with our parents as young, freshly graduated reporters. I drove for an hour north to Rahway one Saturday to go into New York on the train with her for an afternoon. Another weekend she came down to my town and I took her to New Hope, Pa. for a day.

I kept my fantasies to myself and these were nice pleasant times. But there wouldn't be too much more beyond those occasions. By the fall, there'd been gossip flying around the office about V and Tom, and V and I too, I guess. On another night with Tom and some of the other guys, he bragged about dating V. I don't know if he knew my interest, but maybe he did and was trying to shake me up.

So, one very cold day, after work, V and I walk in to a pizza place on Somerville's main street. Things were good until we sat down. My spirits were up as I ordered slices. After a quick few minutes, we had our slices and sodas on trays. V took a bunch of napkins from the dispenser and blotted the grease off her slice.

-I've never seen anybody do that before, I said.

-I don't want all that oil, it's bad. I don't want to get fat.

-You're not fat … I mean, you don't have to worry about that.

A clumsy compliment. We sit down. She curls up her slice, folding it up and down the middle so the cheese is inside. I pick up mine whole, take a bite of the end. After a few bites, she said,

-This is exactly what I didn't want to get into.

-What do you mean?

-I dated a guy at my last job and it didn't go well. I had to get out of there. I was lucky to get the job here, and now the same thing is happening here.

She hung her head down.

-What do you want to ask me?

-Did you go out with Tom?

I thought I was righteous asking that question like an interrogator. I was upset.

-That's exactly what I didn't want to happen.

-What do you mean?

She struggled with her thoughts for a minute.

-I don't want to be the reason why there are bad feelings between people at work.

She paused.

-So, I can't go out with you again. Yeah, he's crass, I didn't end up liking him, but I thought I'd give him a chance. But it's going to create problems if I see you again out of the office.

Disappointed, I slumped back in my chair.

-Why does that have to matter?

-You don't understand, this is your first job. You don't know what happens.

-What happens?

-You get less respect. I don't want to be gossiped about again, or seen as a joke who's not serious.

-Why would anyone think that? Why should that matter?

-It does to me.

I drop it. I can see I'm not going to convince her. I resign myself to play out the rest of the time with her, having small talk, or something, but I can feel myself getting down.

"Goodbye," December 1996

I've packed my car to hit the road for a three-hour drive to York, Pa., a small town where I'd start a new job the next week.

Just a few days before, my coworkers threw me a farewell party at Jack O'Connor's, a giant barn of an Irish pub and restaurant on Route 22 in Bridgewater. But now, I'm parked at the low one-story bunker newspaper office building, where we'd worked, to meet V and say goodbye.

My anger and disappointment about what happened between us two years before at the newspaper had receded. But I was firmly in the friend zone with her, so I wasn't going to be declaring "I love you."

We'd eventually talked again after that impasse. I'd told V I was trying to get a better job elsewhere, especially New York City. She'd clue me in to the primitive Internet job sites of that time – Career Builder and maybe Monster, I think. She'd bring me printouts of job listings. These sites turned out to be the building blocks for the start of my career as a writer and editor at newspapers, sending me to a couple small markets, the first of which would be the one I was headed to in Pennsylvania.

-I'm still so nervous. It's a long way to go, I tell V.

-You'll be fine. Don't worry.

-When I went to try out for this job, I thought, this is impossible, where is this place? And it's going to be a long drive to get there. And now I'm actually going there for good.

-This won't be forever either, you'll see.

-I don't know. I really wanted to be going to New York, not old York, and I'm not.

-You'll get there.

-How?

-You'll see. You have more nerve and ambition than you realize.

-Okay, I say.

I feel wound up and bursting with worry, but also mentally exhausted. I feel compelled to get in the car and drive off, but I don't want to yet. I'm looking down at my feet, and V says, come here, putting her arms out to give me a hug.

-Okay, I murmur, and I hug her back, snapped out of my blues for a minute by getting to touch her. I do rein it in from getting creepy though, to my credit. She lets go and then I do and step back and catch my breath.

-Well, I've gotta go now, I say, wishing I didn't have to.

-Don't worry so much, she said.

Zocalo, Grand Central Station, 2004

It's fall of 2004. I've done my time in the minor leagues of journalism and have now been in New York for over five years. I reconnected with V a year or two prior, after one difficult breakup, looking for a familiar friend. We'd meet for coffee during a workday sometimes, as we weren't that far from each other in Midtown East. So far in New York, I'd had a couple short relationships. The one that just ended a month or two before really stung.

V and I liked going to Zocalo, a Tex-Mex themed place in the basement food halls of Grand Central Station. This time, I'd convinced myself that after all those strike-outs, I should take a swing at something with V. I was going to propose … that if neither of us was married by 40, we should get together. How romantic.

I let that exact spineless proposal spill out of my mouth during dinner with V.

-That's ridiculous, she said.

-What's so ridiculous about it? It makes perfect sense.

She shook her head, not knowing what to say, whether she was puzzled or offended.

-You can't make hypothetical proposals like that. People have feelings, you know, she added with a smirk.

-But, but, but, I stammered, this way we know we'd have each other. It's a good thing, don't you see?

V laughs, baffled.

-I don't think so, she says, still laughing.

And the subject gets changed, and dinner continues on.

Chicago, 2007

The embarrassment of that half-assed proposal, like the days at the New Jersey newspapers, also receded with time.

Enough that we could comfortably go on a sightseeing trip to Chicago together. By this time, I'd accepted finally that I shouldn't press any more for a relationship. That might have helped make things more comfortable between us.

We were out on a boat in the middle of Lake Michigan at night. It was a tourist excursion, a big boat that began its cruises going through the locks at the mouth of the Chicago River to get out onto the lake. It's a June summer night, but it's still as cold as winter.

V and I were enjoying the city, seeing a Cubs game, going to concerts in the Blues Festival, and staying in the regal Palmer House hotel in the Loop, sleeping on either side of a giant king size bed with a lot of room between us.

Out on the windy and chilly lake, dark water all around us, far off from the shore, looking back at the lights of the skyline, I ask V if she's cold and wants to "huddle up." She nods.

We sit like that for most of the cruise, my arms wrapped around her as she leans back into me. We sit quietly, watching the lights, not speaking.

"Non-Magnanimous," 2008

I get an email from V telling me that she has met a guy, actually her boss in the workplace, and that they are dating now. Somehow I was turning shitty again about this. I don't write back for a few days.

I'm home alone one night and I get a call from V.

-Let's get together sometime, she says, and you'll get to meet Jack.

-Can't we just catch up?

-To me, this would be catching up. I think you'll like him.

-I don't know about that.

-You'll see.

Some months later, V meets me for a drink after work one day, quickly before she's headed home. They're living together now.

-You really don't want to meet Jack?, she asks.

I simper, unenthusiastic, saying "I guess I could."

Resignation and disappointment flashes over V's face.

Restaurant in midtown, 2018

Four years after that, we went to each other's weddings in the same summer. I imagined we would socialize often, meeting up in Manhattan. Life got busy, I got occupied with grad school on top of my job, and then we had our daughter in 2014. Or was I forgetting that I had not been accepting of her new relationship at first? Even though I went to the wedding? Or was that all in my head? Was it just being busy and too far away to get together?

I had high hopes for a couples' friendship. They lived out in Connecticut. I'd sometimes try to pin them down for a date, but after a few tries, I gave up for awhile. Then other events took over my life, as you'll see, and I couldn't give any attention to couples' socializing when my own "couple-dom" was in doubt. To this day, I'm still learning that people's lives only have so much bandwidth. I know I can get too pushy about that. Anyway, so this prospective couples' friendship with V and Jack faded without a sound.

Four years or more passed, until the beginning of 2018. There we were, meeting for brunch in the city, about six years since we'd last seen each other. We have Moxie in tow, it's been about a year and a half into my efforts to reform my issues.

V and Jack are marveling about how well behaved Moxie is.

-She's really not like this all the time, I say.

-Well, I imagine that might be the case, she replies, but I'm just trying to give you both a compliment.

-OK, I reply, chastened. I'm taken aback and realize I'm acting snotty or condescending. I take that embarrassed, bad feeling about this away with me and chasten myself about it later.

Dark And Sticky

"Something in me, dark and sticky," – Peter Gabriel,
"Digging In the Dirt"

My dark and sticky things were sexual dysfunction, and
ambition and determination to build a career as a writer.
In the mid- to late 1990s, I moved around for short runs
(no more than two years each) at newspapers in York, Pa.
and Daytona, Fla., building up experience. I didn't think of
it that way at those times. I was grabbing for better work,
but also motivated by dissatisfaction with where I was and
the people around those places. I'd escape the previous
place, then be dissatisfied with the next one, decide it
sucked and I had to get out, and that pushed me on to the
next place to repeat that pattern. This felt like it mattered
so much, but the more important and beneficial result
was that it built up my resume – to be good enough to
eventually get to New York.

While at the weekly newspapers in Somerville, N.J.,
I got an interview with one of the daily papers in York,
Pa. For two or three days before I had to go out to York,

I stewed about whether to even try for the job and go through with the interview. I doubted whether I should go further away from New York, as well as everything I knew from my home area in New Jersey. I feared going somewhere unknown.

I had a friend Andy from the weekly papers. We spoke on the phone during those couple days. I told him my anxieties about going to York, and he gave me a pep talk. He described the opportunity in less absolute terms and made it seem less scary, just something to try. This steadied me and made it possible to push past that undiagnosed anxiety.

I don't recall carrying the same fears when it came to trying for opportunities in New York, because that's what I really wanted, not the local newspaper jobs. The fear of change about New York would only kick in later due to other circumstances piled on top of simply making a job change.

Studies have said 37 to 42 percent of Americans never move further than an 18-mile radius from where they grew up. Now I live within that radius, but I spent about 25 years living in either other states or at least 50 miles away. I'm part of the other half who showed determination and drive, and got outside the average radius.

Making the move back inside that sheltering radius in 2019, disappointed to have left New York, I took our daughter to the street where I grew up, with its modest but nice houses. It looked much smaller than I remember it. Most of the events of my first 15 years took place on that little street. It made up most of my world. Only rarely do I appreciate how unlikely it was that someone from this street could have gone and existed in New York City for 20 years.

The Loneliest Saturday Nights

York, Pa., Market Street, about 11:30 on a
Saturday night in January 1998.

I speed down the back stairwell of the two-story newspaper office and fly out the door into the parking lot.

A couple of the other editors huddle close together having a smoke on a little raised cement ramp by the exit. I sense them there but don't turn back, and they don't pause or say anything. I don't wave or say good night. I make a beeline for my car, an aqua Dodge Shadow compact, and peel out of the lot, or as much as a four-cylinder engine can peel out from anywhere. From the side alley entrance to the lot, I turn right on to Market Street heading west for the five minute ride home.

The drive home goes along Market Street past a few blocks of storefronts and two or three story office buildings, then past two or three story houses. These houses were built pretty close together, maybe even before

131

World War I. They remind me of the houses in inner city Trenton, N.J. near the suburbs where I grew up.

Several more blocks after those houses, I turn left onto a one-way side street, then make two more right turns on one-way streets to get to the side of the house where I live. The front of the house is on Market Street, so I've gone around a big block to get to the side, because of all the one-way streets. Getting out of my car, I trudge up the light metal fire-escape style stairs to my second floor apartment in the three-story house. This entrance opens in to the kitchen in the back of the apartment. There's a front door of the apartment to stairs down to Market Street, but I rarely come and go that way. A weird neighbor lives downstairs, and the apartment above mine is empty.

I drape my heavy coat over a chair, then sit at my computer desk just past the kitchen, across from the table in what passes for a dining room. I press the power button on the desktop computer unit under the desk, and pick up the keyboard off the unit. Pulling the keyboard out by its coiling phone cord, I set it on the small space in front of the monitor on the desk. Then I run to the living room, which is in the middle of this railroad-style apartment. I turn on the 13-inch color TV that sits on a card table across from a beat-up, stiff couch that came with the apartment. I switch to the channel for NBC and fiddle with the rabbit ears, so I can hear Saturday Night Live from my seat in front of the computer. If something sounds funny, I might go watch.

The computer boots up and I sign in to AOL to see if any hometown friends or people from the last job in N.J. are on the IM chat. The middle-aged lady who wrote columns for the Jersey papers wrote me a catch up email. My cousin Ben from Philly is on the IM chat. But I don't feel like reading the email or IM'ing right now.

Instead, I'm thinking about checking out the girls appearing in primitive live stream video on the website I found, where I can type instant messages to them. But mostly, I just watch the girls until they bounce me out for not going to a private paid chat with them. I flip around. Some of the editors at work were going for a drink after deadline, but I didn't want to be social. I craved being solitary at home like this.

I think about just watching SNL instead, or chatting with my cousin, but I'm not in a laughing mood. I'm not in a mood to pour my heart out to anybody, either, which is sometimes what I do with my cousin Ben. So I stay at the desk, touching myself over the crotch of my pants, watching girls on the screen. There's very little car traffic sound from Market Street at this hour, and no one hanging out on the side street, like I sometimes hear. The kitchen has a lot of windows, including a big one in the outside door. If someone came up the steps, they would be able to see where I sit at the desk. Sometimes I get afraid of that happening while I sit like this, stroking myself, so I keep my ears open.

No one's going to see me in this spot, I decide, and I've gotten very hard from watching my favorite girl, who's logged in tonight. I don't type anything on the IM to her, but pull my dick out and continue stroking.

Where had this compulsive masturbation come from? At this point, it was loneliness. It wasn't quite addiction, but it was dysfunction to prefer this to being social and maybe actually meeting someone. Eventually, it would creep toward addiction, under much different circumstances, perhaps motivated by a desire to have some of that familiar loneliness again – but not because of that.

Yet my dysfunction did for a while mutate into addiction. I turned sexy videos, porn and strip clubs into a drug. I became addicted to that drug and abused it. I'd built on the first tastes I had as a teenager and made it the gateway to harder and harder stuff.

Daytona, Fla., winter 1999.

On nights off from my nighttime copy editing job at the Daytona daily newspaper, I'd gone to Club Juana, a strip club in Orlando. I'd sometimes go to more than one on the same night, hitting Club Juana, then another one, Rachel's. At Rachel's, I got to like one of the strippers so much that I thought I could transcend reality and get to see her outside the club, but she shut that down.

I had heard Club Juana on Saturday nights had a special thing where guys from the audience could bid to wrestle with the girls in whipped cream. Given my fetish for wrestling in substances, I had to see this.

I got on the phone to the head of the copy desk at work at about 2 that afternoon, but got his voicemail. I knew he wouldn't be in yet. Feeling guilty about what I was going to do, I was so ashamed that I didn't even call out sick like a normal person – by speaking to the boss and faking a sore throat. I just left a voicemail like a coward. Of course, in pre-cell phone days, I wasn't going to be home to answer the phone if he called back, which would have made my tale of illness less credible.

Still, this was a big leap for me because I prided myself on strong commitment to work at my jobs and not calling out sick unless I was severely ill. I'd often tough it out if I had a bad cold or a flu, beyond all reason.

*   *   *

I pulled up to the club after a drive of 45 minutes or more. On these long drives to the seedy side of Orlando, my anticipation would build – just like it had when I went to strip clubs in New Jersey. The front of Club Juana looked squat and ugly, but over the front doors, it had an outsized theater marquee sign topped with the club name in big neon script. I sat away from the stage, to avoid getting hit up immediately for tips. I spotted a stripper I'd seen before there, a sexy blonde with a short bob of a haircut. She always acted enticing, putting out a lively, party vibe.

I asked if she would be in the wrestling later.

-Sure, you gonna bid on me?

-Definitely.

She slides her hand down my chest and brushes her legs against mine.

I'm charged up and beside myself with excitement.

The bidding starts and I bid $50 for this fantasy, but the amount soon gets too high for me, $100 or more. I'm disappointed that I couldn't get in there with the hot blonde. It's a small consolation to watch her and some of the other girls on stage with the winning bidder, getting all covered in whipped cream, but it gave me a stimulating mental image to file away. I'll carry this one through my drive all the way back home with an unrelenting hard-on.

The next morning at home, the phone rings. It's my boss asking where I'd been. He hadn't found the voice mail for hours, well into my shift. He'd been getting by without me there or found someone to pick up my slack. I mumbled that I thought leaving the message was enough, and a weak "sorry." He was left taking the middle ground – one "misunderstanding" wasn't a firing offense – and told me if it came up again, to make sure I actually spoke to him.

Joe and I Are Tight

Sometimes, I still recall what an ex-girlfriend told me as I was about to leave York, Pa. in 1998 for another job.

"Remember 'Say Anything?' When Lili Taylor won't stop thinking about Joe? And they tell her, 'don't talk to Joe.' You won't walk away from whatever's bothering you. You gotta stop talking to Joe."

Months later, in Daytona, Florida, I found myself doing exactly that. Working a nighttime shift, getting home after midnight, keyed up and wide awake, I'd try to get myself to go to sleep. I'd lay in bed, going through my frustrations in my head. The Daytona apartment seemed big at the time. It looked like a townhouse, with stairs to an upstairs bathroom and bedroom, but that's all the second level had. The first floor had only a kitchen, no bathroom. I had that same small TV, but sprung for cable and HBO, which sucked me in to "The Sopranos" right from its start.

I tried to start a relationship with a co-worker at the new job, but that didn't seem to click. I'd start telling myself how hopeless it was ever going to be to find and have a girlfriend. I couldn't get any job in New York like I'd been trying to do from afar. I removed myself much further away from there by coming to Daytona and wondered how I'd ever even get back to the Northeast.

Most nights after work, I'd come home and go right up to bed, but I had my desk and computer up there, with dial-up internet. One night, I'd found out that the co-worker I went out with two or three times was now dating someone else from work. I trudged up the steps, undressed and got into bed, shut the lights.

-"Why can't I have that? I can't believe she chose that guy. He's a goof and has no substance," I started in with myself, in my head.

-Why did you like her so much, anyway? She's kind of nerdy.

-I guess she reminds me of myself.

Dating her was like dating my mirror image, like the "Seinfeld" episode with Janeane Garofalo playing a male version of him, but as his girlfriend.

All the more reason why the girl from work should have been with me.

-You're angry, my "Joe" tells me.

-Yeah, I'm angry. It's not fair, why can't I get the girl?

-You act like a creep. And you're exuding that depression and sadness at the job.

-I don't care. I don't want to be there. I don't want to be here either.

-You can do something else. You're not going to get to sleep. So turn on the computer.

I turn on the bedside lamp and throw on a t-shirt. I sit at the computer, browsing sexy photos of women from the primitive pre-Google search engines. And I look to see if any of my old friends are on AOL IM this late. Just like Saturday nights in York, Pa.

I find a user profile page somewhere, which shows a picture of a woman wearing a black and white striped one-piece swimsuit, cut off below her face. I e-mail her and she responds with some flirty replies, e-mailing back in nearly real time during those late night hours. I keep that picture in view on the screen as I end up jerking off.

In hindsight much later, it dawned on me this woman was probably really a guy, as hard up for gratification as I was. I ignored obvious signs this person wasn't who they claimed to be.

Anyway, this exchange didn't dispel any of Joe's influence. In bed in the dark, I circled over and over the same despairing, self-flagellating thoughts in my head. I made myself more and more depressed. It kept me from sleeping. I couldn't stop thinking these thoughts and beating myself up. There were many nights like this. I could only muster a weak challenge to this compulsion.

I couldn't stop talking to Joe.

*   *   *

Where did my incessant talks with Joe lead me? After a few months, it was to the hospital, thinking I had appendicitis, but it turned out to be nothing but anxiety and depression. They told me to go see a psychiatrist. So one sunny morning, I arrived at a medical office building near the hospital for an appointment.

The waiting room had no receptionist. A diminutive Filipino woman emerged, introduced herself and showed me in. She wore a muted purple business suit, a paisley scarf, large glasses and dark black straight hair in a bob. We sat down. After the formalities, she asked me to tell the whole story of how I ended up in the hospital. Listening, she nodded her head. Then she started picking me apart, but with a neutral tone, not aggressive, but clinical.

-Do you have trouble sleeping?

-Yes.

-What happens when you try to go to sleep?

-"I can't get to sleep. I keep thinking," I say, and relate how I would ruminate about my situation in my head when I can't sleep, and get more and more upset.

She probed with more questions about this spiraling compulsion. She started explaining how serotonin works in the brain. I comprehended the facts but didn't understand right away how this related to my issues.

-What you have is depression, the doctor said.

-What does that mean? I know I feel down a lot, but what does depression mean?

-It's a condition, an illness. But we can treat it.

This was the moment when I first got a name for what was happening to me, and also the beginning of a years-long road to learn how to cope with it. Being told this by a psychiatrist left me numb at the time, but as the knowledge sunk in, it became a revelation to have an answer and a reason for everything that had been going on in my head, in my thoughts.

Anyway, the doctor handed me samples of Buspar and Zoloft, plus prescriptions for both. I found out later that Phil Hartman's wife was taking Zoloft, and I guess that wasn't working too well. The Zoloft ended up upsetting my stomach, so then she had me stick to Buspar. From there, I was off and running on a pharmacological odyssey that would last a lifetime.

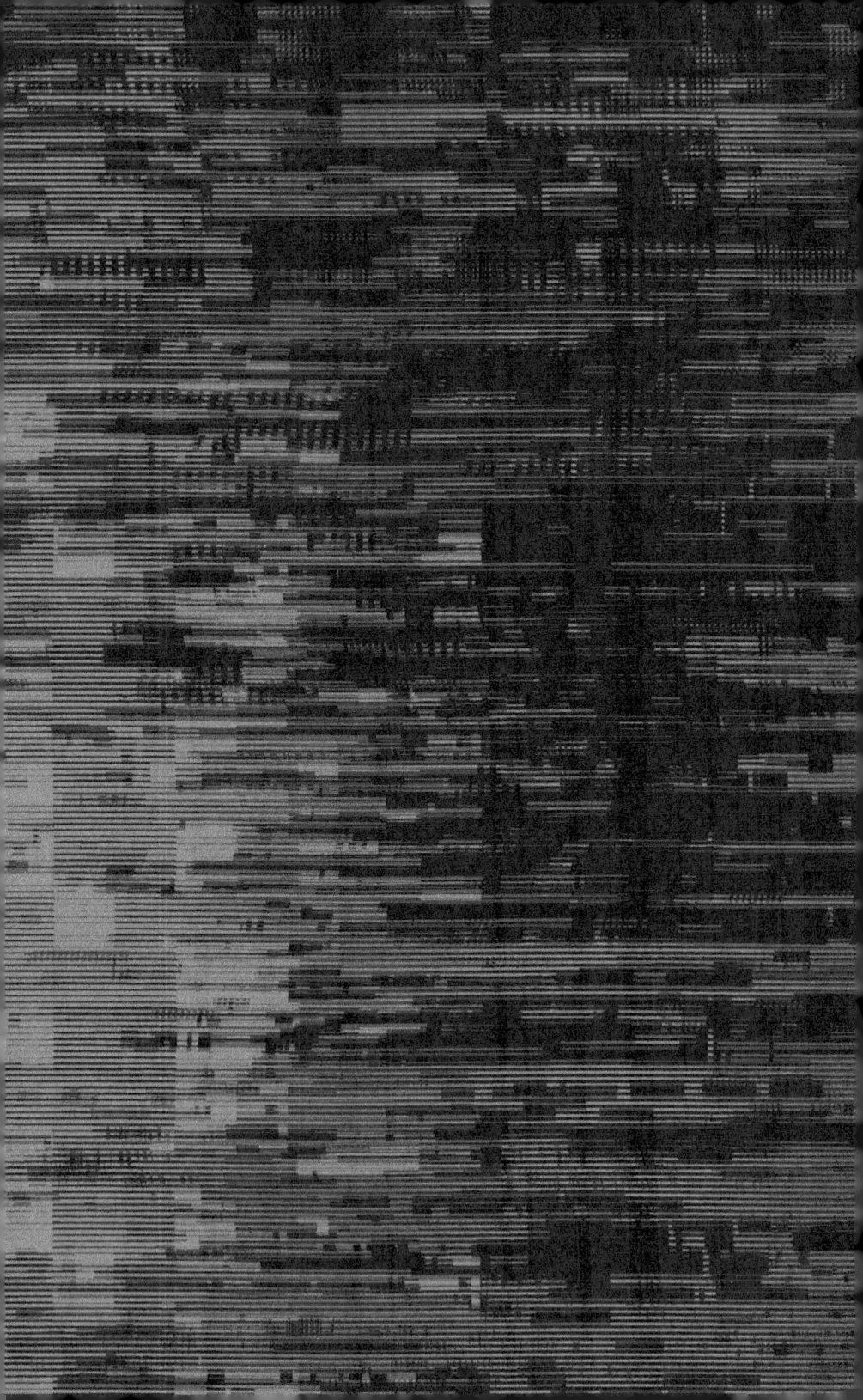

A Psychiatric Maze in NYC

Not too long after this episode, I turned down a job offer in New York. I'd actually flown back to NJ and went into the city for the interview, but when they offered me the job, I began agonizing all over again, worried that making another abrupt shift would fuck up my fragile psyche. Partly out of fear of failure, apprehension about how I would make the move and find a place to live in New York, and also the thought that maybe I should stay put to get better, I went back and forth over the course of a few days about whether to take the offer or not.

As much as I knew I wanted to be in New York and yearned for that, I thought it was the right decision to avoid psychological stress when I was trying to get better mentally. This was the safe choice, and I made a lot of safe choices in my 20s that didn't help me much. I didn't think I had the love and support of my parents. I couldn't articulate to them my fears about making that move. I was also afraid to fail at the job I ended up declining.

When I flew in for the New York job interview, I landed at the little local airport, a short drive from my parents' house. They came to pick me up. After that phantom appendicitis, seeing them waiting for me moved me deeply, and I wrapped my arms around them in a big, long hug.

*   *   *

About a year later, I did get another opportunity in New York, and that time I took it. By that time, I'd gotten good at the job in Daytona, and I'd steadied myself a bit. I'd been able to fly back to NJ again and go into the city for an interview. But I wasn't 100%.

My Daytona friend, the older guy, had to urge me to push hard for an in-person interview, after I got interest in my application for a copy editor job. The job opportunity surfaced right when I had already planned a visit north. It was serendipity.

I followed his advice and booked an interview at their office. A few weeks later, they hired me, and I set to packing up for another move, first to my childhood home, then five weeks later, to Jersey City.

The scene I remember most is finally getting my car hitched to the U-Haul truck to start the drive north from Florida. This time I was doing the drive alone. My plan was to get as far as I could and then find a hotel for the night, then complete the second half the next day. I made it to the northern part of North Carolina, in eight hours or so, before a big rainstorm hit. I figured it would be best if I stopped. I found a Homewood Suites hotel.

I hardly remember the driving itself anymore, just the stops. I ate at a McDonalds next to the hotel, then hit the road again. I stopped again in Maryland, not too far from where I went to college. I had difficulty driving the truck around some narrow winding roads there. The rest is a blur.

The other thing I remember about this transition time is the commutes into Manhattan from Ewing and Hamilton every day, for about 90 minutes on the train both ways. I'd get back to the house at around 8 pm, exhausted from an eight-hour workday (or longer), plus three hours of commuting.

After the temporary 5-week stop back "home," Mark joined me to move again in October 1999, this time up the NJ Turnpike, to the apartment in Jersey City. I made a joke I'm not proud of now, in context. It was funny at the time I guess. I put on a Middle Eastern voice as the New York skyline came into view. Since we were driving a Ryder truck, I said, "Which way is your World Trade Center?" And we laughed.

I was stronger, but getting settled working in New York still stressed me, and over time, my prescription regimen got shaken up and needed adjustments. The psychiatrist in Daytona had also fulfilled the function of a therapist, talking with me for an hour every time. So I assumed that every psychiatrist did that.

The first one I had in New York, Dr. P., only spent about 15 minutes or so in appointments. I started to wonder why he wasn't discussing things more in depth with me, and finally asked him. He told me that's not what psychiatrists usually do. He said I need to find a psychologist, a therapist, other than him. I went through

145

two or three different ones those first several years in New York. I'd feel like they weren't helping, and drift off. Then another crisis would come along, and push me to seek a new one.

One way or another, I kidded myself that I was fine, that I wasn't depressed or anxious anymore. I told Dr. P. that. So he took me off the medications. Psychiatrists and therapists can only be as good as what you tell them. After a month or two, it all came roaring back. I'd been dating my second girlfriend of my time in New York. Walking in the west 30s in midtown one day in an upset state, it struck me that I needed the medication again. I made another appointment with Dr. P. But I wasn't content with him.

*   *   *

The next psychiatrist I had, Dr. G. (different last name than the childhood one), I saw for seven or eight years, from about 2003 to 2010. Those years spanned various girlfriends, then finally meeting my wife-to-be. Dr. G. helped me a lot for a good part of that time. He guided me through a big change in medications, to a mix of two put together that ended up being more effective. Once he brought me to that mix, he modulated dosages up and down depending on my feedback about how I was feeling.

Seeing Dr. G. ended abruptly. He decided he wasn't going to accept insurance anymore and only see patients at full price. I couldn't afford that. I felt let down and disappointed.

After Dr. G., I went through three more psychiatrists before leaving New York, each for less time than the previous one. They all worked off the medication mix Dr. G. had started, with minor dosage adjustments from time to time.

Accelerating A Porn Habit (Jersey City/NYC)

Seeing these psychiatrists and therapists, I hardly ever divulged anything about my masturbatory compulsion or addiction. That gradually got worse as the years passed in New York. In my 20s, I had indulged a lot at times in sexy videos and strip clubs, in a way like someone who drinks too much but hasn't completely turned into a full-blown alcoholic.

Here's how I eventually ended up there. In 2002 or 2003, I returned to buying erotic wrestling videos. Back in 1997 or '98, desiring self-improvement, I threw out my videotape collection. The videos I bought this time, though, on DVDs, went further than the videotapes. The women's wrestling would morph into hardcore lesbian porn. Then I started getting the mixed erotic wrestling DVDs. With guys in these videos, the sex got more aggressive.

I hadn't wanted to see hardcore sex before, and at first I turned off those DVDs before they got to that point, but eventually that barrier snapped, and I started liking that too. I'd been on my own for longer. After the first two years in New York of living with roommates in Jersey City, I got my own studio apartment so I had privacy that I hadn't had since the small towns before New York.

While in Jersey City, I started going on dates and having girlfriends over in my bedroom in the shared apartment. During that time, I was starting to connect with women. I didn't have a TV in my room, and computers couldn't handle much video yet back then, so I wasn't falling back on porn like I would after leaving there for a studio apartment in late 2001.

The mixed wrestling videos were a gateway to even harder-core stuff, like kink videos showing women bound, tied and gagged, and videos of guys ejaculating on girls. The common theme was aggression or simulated violence against women, or humiliation of women. These videos were all performances, however extreme the actions depicted. The women looked like porn performers in some way. That's not to say these women who appeared in these videos weren't suffering any kind of psychological damage at all from these performances, but the way the scenes played out read as a performance of some kind.

With every relationship that broke up, which happened about once a year or so for those few years, I'd escalate how much I watched porn and how extreme the porn got.

The subject matter stayed a fantasy for me, though. I wasn't trying to act this stuff out in real life. I thought

150

about that, but the cost deterred me. Even before coming to New York, I'd found a website for a company in New York that, for hundreds of dollars, would set you up to wrestle a girl in private, but there wasn't a promise or a hint of actual sex being part of the transaction. Maybe you got to go jerk off afterward.

Sometimes, I'd try introducing light versions of what I was watching into real experiences with women, without as much of the hardcore or aggression. But that became no match for my preference for the extreme simulations I saw in the porn. I'd prefer that to real life, and go unsatisfied with real-life sexual activity. Another thing I didn't realize was that the anxiety and depression medication were dulling sexual stimulation so much that it helped push me to more extreme material to stimulate anything. This wasn't the only reason for the addiction, but it contributed to it.

Is This Sociopathy?

The high testosterone of youth, in my 20s, was the foundation for the twisted and anti-social desires of those years.
The dulling effects of medication, instead of stopping that
behavior, pushed it in a different direction.

In the late 1990s, in what little dating life I had, I'd be
petty about things like whose turn it was to buy the meal.
I'd believe pickiness like this was just a good gauge for
how much a girl cared about me. This was a self-protective
armor gone astray and undermining me instead of helping
me. The result was I'd come off like an asshole, and no
relationship would last.

This attitude hadn't changed much once I got the
New York and started having some success with dating.
The primitive dating websites of the early 2000s helped
break the ice and greatly increased the possibilities for
an introvert like me. Dating sites made a lot of first dates

possible, and a few successive relationships of less than a year each. My social life and my personal focus revolved around that for about six years or so.

I can point to many little failures from these years. There was one girlfriend who mentioned things that were bothering her but would say she didn't want to discuss them. If I cared, even if she kept declining, I would have pressed her to share and tried to help or be supportive. But I couldn't be that caring guy, that great boyfriend. I was all in my own head, and just concerned with myself and what I wanted. And, of course, there was all that sexual self-stimulation I'd be busy with and wouldn't share.

Another girlfriend told me she an issue with co-dependency. I wasn't sympathetic. I'd mockingly dismiss it – not to her face – but in talking to friends. I didn't understand what co-dependence meant or what kind of problem it could be, much less how a couple with co-dependency issues could work on those to keep a relationship healthy.

I've gotten better—maybe I'm just bad with empathy now, rather than completely terrible. Still uneasy and awkward trying to be empathetic.

But back to testosterone. In a lot of research and reading I did about the sexual addiction issues I had, one noted clinical psychologist wrote that men with more testosterone are less interested in commitment. That seems obvious, but it could explain why I never got past the honeymoon phase of a new relationship—purposeful, if unconscious self-sabotage.

From Jersey City To NYC

My first two years living in Jersey City (and working in New York) finished on a cloudy, windy and cold night at the end of September 2001. When the wind shifted, you could still pick up the smell of human remains from the Trade Center site across the Hudson River. On the concrete plaza outside the high rise where I'd lived, a few friends helped me load all my stuff into a truck. As we were finishing up, some light bags and things almost got blown away. I freaked out, bolting after them, just barely catching them before they blew off.

The time in this apartment started with high hopes. It ended grimly, even without accounting for 9/11 having just happened right across the river. But I had high hopes again for where I'd be moving to. That was the Jewish neighborhood of Riverdale in the Bronx, where my girlfriend at that time lived. (I'd ended up staying the night at her place on 9/11 when it was impossible to get back to Jersey City).

155

The Jersey City apartment had three bedrooms and was on the sixth floor of a building that had more than 20 floors. I'd gotten the lease with an old colleague from the Jersey newspapers who had also just gotten a job in New York that fall of 1999. The view wowed us. To get it, we found a third roommate who we didn't know before.

In our late 20s, we should have known better but were too trusting. We didn't check the guy's references. He turned out to be an awful deadbeat, ignoring rent, until we finally kicked him out. Of course, this asshole took us to court or arbitration or something. He had no real case against us, and there wasn't any penalty for us. The consequences were personal, because it fractured the relationship with my colleague and other roommate. He didn't like my harsh stance with the deadbeat guy, who moved out before the end of that year's lease. Then we replaced him, and when my colleague left, I then got a new third roommate to replace the colleague so I could stay there another year. I moved into the bedroom that had its own bathroom at that point, which used to be my colleague's.

Anyway, dealing with the deadbeat brought out my aggressive side. I got so angry that I could think of nothing but how to get him. There was a Friday night in April 2000 where I was the only one home, stewing after he hadn't paid rent. A switch flipped in my head and I decided, "If his rent isn't paid, he's no longer entitled to privacy." I went in his room and found his answering machine on the floor. I listened to the messages to him that were left on it.

There were two or three voice mails where people had left their phone numbers. On a mission, I called them, told them who I was and that I was trying to find the guy because he hadn't paid his rent. One of them might have been a family member, who dismissed me. Another was someone who also had been wronged by the guy in some way. I don't remember all the details.

Before that, the next week, I was ready to go after him at his workplace, even writing something I was going to fax to his employer. The intention was that his colleagues might see it, to embarrass him.

Some days later, he returned and all three of us were there. The deadbeat gave us some lame excuses. I got wound up all over again, and I must have been deep into watching The Sopranos around then. I yelled at him with a Tony-like cadence and indignation, "You're pissing down my leg and telling me it's raining!"

I was right about the guy's deadbeat nature, but brewing up that much anger, even if it was righteous, just made me aggravated and didn't fix anything.

Much later, I'd recognize how I often took my anger about other issues in my life out on something or someone that I thought was screwing me over. That perception would trigger me unloading all my negative energy about everything onto them and whatever they did. Now I sometimes can stop myself from doing this when I feel it about to happen, but that took many years to achieve.

*   *   *

So, that second year in Jersey City, I had two roommates I didn't know and didn't care to associate with. When I re-signed, I knew I was only buying time and would find somewhere else after another year.

157

Being right on the Hudson waterfront with all its wind and cold in the wintertime, the apartment could get cold and uncomfortable, since it was in a newer building and lacked a central furnace. Instead, it had cheap hybrid heat/AC units in the bedrooms that couldn't counteract all the drafts from its large, tall windows. The apartment had a concrete outdoor deck to enjoy the view, but I didn't make the most of that, and wasn't out on it much. The lack of warmth wasn't helped by simulated hardwood floors that we didn't carpet.

The apartment I moved to in Riverdale was the opposite, as far as keeping warm went. It had steam radiator heat that I'd leave turned all the way up. Combined with blinds I always kept shut, I made it a cocoon.

In the Jersey City apartment, I had come to behave that way – self-isolating, keeping to myself and staying in my bedroom, hardly ever hanging out in the common room. That was especially true in the second year with the new roommates, and with a bedroom that had its own bathroom. So, in this apartment with its fantastic view, I'd taken to burrowing into my dark, secluded hiding place, with dark blue curtains over the windows.

After the roommate fiasco that first year, I headed right toward another crisis that blew up in my face. I volunteered for local politics and won a seat on a Democratic party committee. I also organized neighbors in the building with grievances against the management, but dropped the ball on following through with any of that. I'd host people in the apartment and annoy the old colleague and roommate further, also spiking my anxiety with more tensions with him. With the politics stuff, I thought I was fighting a good fight for people as an activist, but I'd quickly getting disappointed, which didn't exactly help with depression.

Caught up in all of that, I'd fallen out of the habit of online sexual gratification for a little while, and didn't start up again until I got the private apartment on my own in Riverdale. In some respects, in that second year in the Jersey City apartment, I did start getting out more, dating and having a social life. It pulled me away from solitary tendencies a little bit.

My plan to move out of Jersey City started before 9/11, so leaving wasn't a reaction to that event. I changed jobs in March 2001, so my commute then had me leaving about 8 or 8:30 a.m., taking the PATH train across the river, then walking to the 4/5/6 subway and taking that to mid-town. I would have been right by the Towers at the time the first plane hit. But that day, I left an hour earlier to go sign my new lease out on Long Island before I went to work.

By that fluke, or a stroke of luck, or an angel looking out for me, I missed being the middle of the carnage. I sat on a LIRR train in Lawrence, N.Y. after signing the lease, expecting to return to the city and work, but starting to hear the news filtering though conversations of passengers around me.

Otherwise, I would have been walking on the plaza outside what became Ground Zero, seeing a lot of the horrors or maybe even being injured or killed from falling debris or burning jet fuel – as some were. I already had been mentally shaky, with psychiatric issues. Having that compounded with 9/11 PTSD could have broken me completely.

The Story of E

I'm stewing in my anger late one weeknight in 2005, a month or two after "E" broke up with me and I'm browsing profiles on jDate. But I just can't get into looking for someone else to date. I'm thinking of all her favorite things, and I start wondering what her jDate password is. I remember she liked a certain classic silent film star, and I guess that might be her password.

And I guessed right.

So I'm in her account, and seeing who she's writing to, and if there's any sign she's seeing anyone new. There isn't much. A couple messages to guys, one talking about setting up a first date. I look at who's on her "likes" list, and the wheels in my head start churning. I want to make her feel as low as she made me feel by breaking it off with me so abruptly, not even in person. I fantasize about sending dirty come-ons to a bunch of guys from her account, and how that would hurt and embarrass her.

The angel and the devil in my head start having a conversation.

-What was so hot when we had sex was the way she'd tell me to "put it in her." I want to message guys from her telling them to "stick your dick in me."

-You can't do that. First, if you cared anything about her at all ever, you would be devastating her.

-I'm so mad. Want to make her pay and hurt like I hurt.

-I'm still talking. Second, there must be some law on the books for this. You could get into big trouble, maybe even get arrested, at least for harassment, if not something worse.

-Okay, okay, you're right.

*　　*　　*

Many months earlier, when we were still together, we were together at her place late one night, after having had some drinks out someplace. I'm on my phone trying to get a refund for movie tickets we bought and didn't go to. I can feel myself getting angry and aggressive with the Fandango operator, when I look over and see E lying on the floor, passed out.

Still I don't hang up immediately, and I sigh. But I get calmer and more polite on the call, wanting to wrap it up, which I finally do once they've credited my card back. A petty George Costanza move indeed. But then I go over to E, and pick her up off the floor and lay her down on the couch. She mumbles and mutters something. I say, in a soft voice, are you OK? Then she snaps out of it, asks what happened? I tell her, you fell asleep on the floor. She laughs a little bit, somewhat embarrassed.

*   *   *

Of the eight months or so dating E, what I remember is
that there were more bad things than good things. But the
bad things that frustrated me were more my fault than
hers. Plus the good memories all have that cloud of it
being a relationship that didn't last, so the good memories
just turn into regrets.

I'd get stuck on petty worries, and didn't show
empathy (something I'm still not so great at). So I came off
as cold and unsupportive. About two or three months into
it, I got annoyed at always checking in with the doorman
of her building, then having to wait to go up to her place. I
kept insisting E give me a key so I could go right up like a
resident there, until she broke down and did.

That key led to good and memorable times though.
We got to talking about turn-ons and I said I thought
about her answering her door to greet me naked.

One night after an improv show at Upright Citizens
Brigade (I had started taking classes there), I called E, who
lived uptown.

-I want to come up and see you, I said.

-Yeah? I really want you to.

-How badly? Would you greet me the way we talked
about?

-I might, she teased.

-Oh god, I can't wait.

-Get up here. Call me when you get off the train.

-And you'll have your clothes off?

-Call when you get up here. Don't use your key.

So I rode the subway uptown, stifling my urges so I
wouldn't have a bulge poking out of my pants while on

163

the train. Same thing while walking to her building. But I couldn't help thinking about her fit body, small but perky and full breasts, cute face and smile, and short but not too short, neck-length hair. Sure, I lusted for all of this about her, but I loved all of this about her too.

I felt a buzz of sexual excitement checking in at her building's front desk, that grew as I got on the elevator. Anticipation of the imminent encounter felt electric.

I rang the doorbell. And E opened it slowly, and all that I just described was there before me. Her being naked while I was still dressed made it all the more thrilling.

*   *   *

I never had the temperament for yoga. E was into it, even going away to a new age retreat while I knew her. Here are the comical attempts:

Doing political volunteering while I was in Jersey City, I met far more people in the building than I would have otherwise. One was a middle-aged yoga teacher who gave classes in one of the community rooms. I went to try it, borrowing a mat.

She led the class speaking in a soothing voice, instructing the students to get into particular positions, like "downward dog," the basic starting one where you're on your knees and elbows, moving forward and back to stretch various muscles. I tried to follow the instructions but would get frustrated trying to hold a stretch long enough or relax in a given position.

The teacher tried to get me to relax with a hand on my back or my arm, but I couldn't control anything and couldn't do what was being asked. I was wired with tension. The second time I went, in the middle of the class, I stopped trying to do any of the activity. I didn't come back again. I beat myself up for not being able to get it and do it. Exactly not the point of doing yoga in the first place.

Now, my wife knows a lot about how to do yoga, but I'm still hopeless at it. I can't follow anybody's instruction about how to move, what to move or where to move it. Getting me to do any particular stretch right—like one that might help my back or legs—means telling me three or four times.

The way I carry myself, to this day, is the opposite of yoga. So it's no surprise that I could never be zen enough with E.

Family Snapshot

-Michael, there is something hard to talk about with my family, E told me one night.

-What is it?

-I can't really talk about it. It's too hard.

My mind went to all sorts of horrible things. Did she have a relative who abused her as a kid? E had told me she was born with the umbilical cord wrapped around her neck, which possibly cut off oxygen in that key moment. She didn't ever come off like she was mentally challenged, but when we were around her family, her siblings seemed to have an overly sympathetic tone that could have stemmed from that knowledge.

Later, I'd meet guys socially who I'd see being much more attuned to their girlfriend's issues. One got back into his ex's life when her father passed, showing so much sympathy and support that they ended up together again, eventually married. I never could bring myself to be this supportive, even seeing it pay off like that. I should have learned it then, but the lesson still didn't stick.

Meanwhile, I reply to E, are you sure?

-Yes, she whispered.

And I let it drop. And let the mystery fester in my own head also.

That was the moment E needed my support, even asking directly for it. I couldn't care enough to push, even a little, to reveal more. To show that I cared and wanted to understand. To show support. I didn't get that this was how people show they care about each other.

Saturday Night Fever

E was dedicated to her work as a casting director for movies and TV. When we started dating, she challenged me, wanting me to confirm I wasn't trying to get acting roles by being with her. I'd just started UCB classes when we met, but I genuinely wasn't trying to go be an actor. That was all about being into comedy and improv, and the vast world of that I'd just started discovering in 2004. E said other guys had dated her just to get a leg up on getting cast as actors. I don't know if I convinced her on that issue, but her work seemed cool and interesting to me. Of course, I never expressed it that way at the time. Strike two.

When I knew her, E was working under other casting directors, and had a boss who was callous and didn't

166

always treat her so well. One Saturday, she had to go in and work the whole day and then some – 10 or 11 hours – because a project had pressing casting demands. While she worked, I was hanging out in her apartment waiting for her. As the day went on, I got more and more upset that she wasn't done yet and back to be with me.

Stewing there, unwilling to just watch TV or DVDs from her shelves, I started plotting when to call or text. It had gotten to be mid-afternoon and I wanted to know when she might be home, expecting we'd get dinner together.

-When can I call, my internal devil asked.

-You called at lunchtime. Don't interrupt her when she's working. You don't want her to get distracted, do you?

-I don't care. She can take a minute to give me some idea of what's going on.

-Why don't you text her and ask if she needs anything, my better angel suggested, even as he knew I wouldn't.

-Why doesn't she tell her boss to divide this shit into two days, or do it during the actual business week, my devilish side shot back.

-Oh, that would be a great idea, the angel said while rolling their eyes.

My wave of anger turned into frustration, then resignation. More hours went by and I didn't hear from E. I went and picked up take out for myself, then came back. Around 8, she called and told me she probably wouldn't get done until 11 that night. She was upset with the situation, I could hear it in her voice. A supportive boyfriend would have asked at this point if he could bring her some take-out, but that was not me.

Dating / Improv

Dating was like improv that I didn't have any training in. I didn't know what to do, so my fallback was to act like it was an interview for the job of boyfriend. I wouldn't let conversation flow and I'd just be trying to tick off the boxes of questions about a date's job, family and time in New York. I pursued women from online dating sites mostly based on their pictures, and if I did get to meet them, and I liked them in person, by the end of my dull, stiff interview-slash-conversation, I would at least feel a vibe that it wasn't going well and they probably wouldn't want to see me again. That signal I could receive, but picking up on signals enough to flirt or improvise in conversation was beyond me.

I'd feel pain and disappointment when these first dates or meet-ups didn't go anywhere, whether the woman was honest and considerate enough to tell me they weren't interested or just ghosted me. Either way, it made no difference. I'd still feel resentment.

*　　*　　*

I love and respect what improv comedy performers do. Before I started my own comedy reviews and interviews website in 2005, I took classes with Upright Citizens Brigade in New York. In the end, these classes were a spark that made me more confident, or at least more playful and fluid in conversations or socially. It was difficult to evolve that way, get past my reserve, but the classes planted that seed. It took a long time – years -- for that ability to find its way into first dates or social interactions.

Improv training has a credo, "don't think," that I had trouble following. I couldn't shut off my over-thinking stuff in scenes that came up in the "Harold" format. That's improv where about eight players line up and two or three at a time might step forward with something to say to each other, which would begin improvised scenes. I'd stand paralyzed in the back line, rarely stepping forward to speak or react. I regret not loosening up and failing to follow the credo. I know I'd be much better at improv now, for what it's worth. When I draw on that experience, I feel more creative. My spirits rise when I think of funny things or have a quick wit in conversations. Remembering the other improv principle of "yes, and," which means listening and reacting by adding something, I like to play this way with Gabi, joking about stuff.

In fact, I probably have the "10,000 hours" that is said to be key to mastering a craft, from all the years of banter with my wife. It's something I forget and I'm not always the most appreciative for, but I recognize that. I got much better at it because of her. The UCB classes were a key to unlock that, or a foundation to build on.

That respect for improv translated into love through our time together. I love and enjoy letting the spark of wit or ideas come into my head and then putting them right out there. I've also got much quicker at that, and removed the filters, apprehension and over-thinking that I once had.

How I Met The Mother

By the time I first met my wife, I'd had several short-term relationships in New York. Despite my wooden and stiff first date game, sometimes I actually did get to a second date. Still, all those first-date disappointments sometimes clawed back whatever confidence or flexibility I'd built. On first meetings, I'd keep a poker face in the conversation. My wife later said that when we first met, I was "very hard to read."

I don't remember many details of when we first met, but I do remember bumbling my big plan when meeting Gabi. The first midtown pub I picked was too crowded and it would have been hard to hear each other in conversation. So I was leading her down the street, trying to think of another place. We popped into another bar I recognized but it was too loud there too. Then we settled on one of the Playwright Taverns in the theater district. Gabi was being agreeable even though I felt I was blowing it.

Later, again, she filled in some blanks I have about that first meeting. She relishes saying she knew I needed an extra push to turn this meeting into something more. As we parted, she touched my arm and said, "call me."

Even without that, I still would have. I do remember that.

Anger, Aggression and Arrogance

Just as it took years to find a relationship that could last, it was also a gradual descent over years stretching from my past into the marriage. I'd finally begin to unpack all of this in therapy at the beginning of 2017, after getting caught in my indulgences the previous fall. I wanted to atone and try to get better. My sexual fantasies and self-gratification had escalated with cam girls, porn and sexting. Gabi and I had a sex life, but we weren't in sync, because all these behaviors that I tried to keep secret got in the way of what should have been. I was preferring that to the real thing.

I first found camgirl sites around 1998 on those lonely Saturday nights and really kicked in to actually spending money on them around 2011 or 2012.

Traveling for work provided opportunity to be alone with these gratifications. The job I had from 2011 to 2016

took me away from home sometimes and gave me opportunities to indulge. I looked forward to going away on
those trips, knowing I'd get to really cut loose with porn
and camgirls. While doing business, being at a conference
or working all day, in the back of my mind, I'd be thinking
about ending my night in a hotel room and doing that.
And in my head, I justified this as OK and not wrong,
since I wasn't doing anything in person with anyone. I
told myself that line was sufficient, but it was too far over
the real line.

I found one camgirl site in 1998, while in York, Pa.,
and browsed it a lot then and during 1999 when I lived
in Florida, but I couldn't bring myself to spend money on
it then. I could get enough simulation from browsing the
camgirl chat rooms to be satisfied. For years after that, I
also got into erotic wrestling porn, in the 2000s, which
held me back from spending on camgirls for awhile. But
eventually, after some years, I bought blocks of "private"
time on that site, using these blocks a very little at a time.

Then I migrated to a different site that charged per
minute of private time with a camgirl, rather than using
pre-bought blocks of private time. This became an outlet
for my aggressive impulses and fantasies. The things I
would write there, in trying to test how receptive they
would be to what I wanted, were misogynistic. But I
would never say or write those things to anyone who
wasn't getting paid to hear it.

Anyway, my M.O. was working myself up into a
heightened state of sexual stimulation by clicking in and
out of different camgirls' rooms. Maybe I'd test some of
them with some chat, drawing out a process of deciding

who to go private with. I tried to screen out camgirls who weren't responsive in free chat, because they would likely ignore my direction in private.

By the time I'd go private with someone, trying not to spend too much money, I'd be primed to come very quickly. It wouldn't take much acting or stimulation by the girl to have me finish. And as soon as I did, I'd click out of the room and shut the meter. I was cheap and nasty.

Rarely, I'd stay in a room longer, for the girl to get me to climax – or linger a bit after that and pay a little more as appreciation.

I also found paid group shows, where you paid a lower flat fee, but the camgirl did what they wanted to for many others paying in $5 or $10 or so, all at once. You could type things to the performer in these, but they wouldn't necessarily pay attention or respond to you. They'd have their routine, dancing, then stripping, then simulating sex acts.

When I thought about writing this book, I dove deep on the question of whether I really had a sex addiction that I was powerless to stop or I was just an arrogant asshole.

There's a psychologist, David Ley, who wrote a book called "The Myth of Sex Addiction." I thought this book might have something to teach me or give me some insight. Ley had something to say about a link between sex and aggression in the evolution of the human brain. I had all that aggression going into instructions to camgirls. The parts of the brain associated with aggression are close to the areas of the brain driving men's erections. Both these actions reside in primitive areas of the brain, sometimes called "reptilian."

I didn't know and couldn't articulate all this biology at the time, but it was the more elevated parts of my brain that rationalized those uncontrolled primal drives. I used my higher intelligence to construct all the dirty messages to camgirls, but the source was the reptilian part of my brain. Ley wrote that humans' survival instinct knows that 40 percent of men have reproduced in history, while 80 percent of women have. Therefore, men had to be aggressive, dominant and hypersexual to get to reproduce. The aggression and arousal areas of the male brain are close together due to an evolution that fuels that instinct.

Instead of being a caveman dragging a woman off to his cave, unacceptable in a society that has evolved higher intelligence, I repressed that kind of drive and urge into my secret activities. The arrogance grew out of that as another construct – a careful effort to justify what I was doing. I made up my own boundaries and my own rules without ever getting agreement on those.

What is rationalization, then? How did the rationalizations I came up with function?

Rationalization as a defense mechanism. I sought to protect myself and my ability to continue every other part of my life without blowing it up. Eventually that failed. The marriage nearly ended once it all got discovered.

Rationalization is self-sabotage. It's also letting emotions drive decisions. My emotions in those times were anger, in whatever form, about any one of many circumstances. I put the anger into the aggressive talk and aggressive arousals.

Rationalization is a compromise solution. I couldn't resolve, on my own, the conflict between my hidden behavior and the upstanding parts of my life. The defense mechanism of my rationalizations made me feel better. But when I got off with a camgirl, immediately afterward, intense guilt and shame followed.

Casual sex, even virtually with camgirls, can make depression increase, and I still had depression. The more I did it, the tougher it got to escape that depression. Then I couldn't do anything to address the issues that bothered me, that fed my depression. I wasn't doing myself any favors.

My defense mechanisms, my rationalizations and my depression all fed and manifested in my arrogance. That arrogance dictated how I would act and what I would do for gratification. The urge to do it felt like an addiction, but I still had agency and an ability to control myself sometimes, so I don't think I can conclude it was actually an addiction. I had free will and could have shown responsibility.

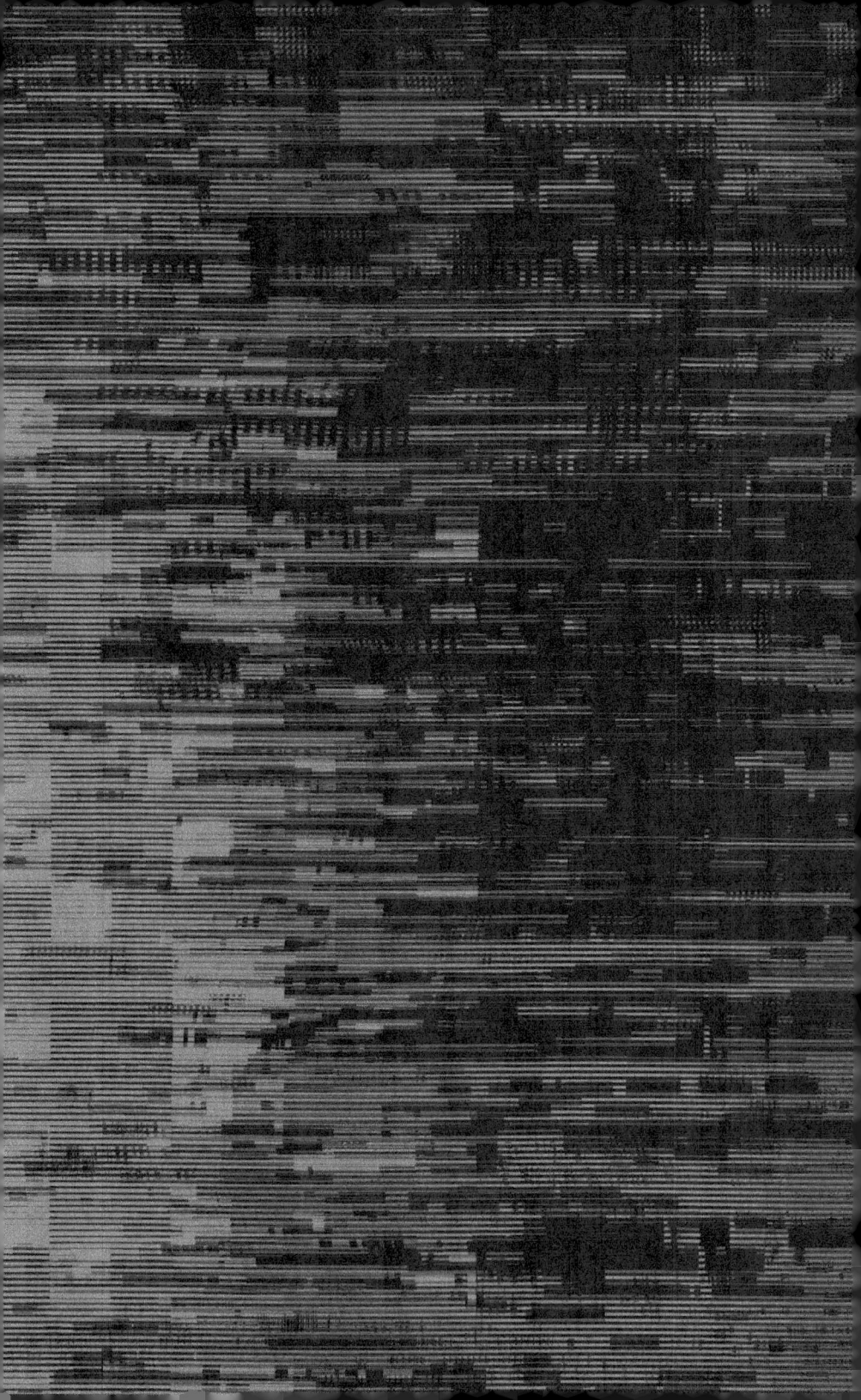

Frenzied

I had many favorite camgirls and had sessions with several different ones over time. And when I'd browse Match or JDate when I was single, most of the time I'd pay attention to a girl's photo first before I even read their profile. I was thinking about attraction and sex before substance. Old friends I knew who settled down young, in their 20s, never experienced online dating like I did.

Browsing camgirls unleashed my id, without any noble goal like a real relationship to constrain me. I'd look at their profile pictures, then at their photo albums, then pop into their room. Some turned up only rarely, some would seem to be there every time I went on to look. Rare appearances by a girl I liked charged me up. Some sat still. Some looked bored. Some performed for the camera, playing with dildoes or dancing like strippers. Some would talk in short disconnected sentences, speaking answers to things guys had typed in the chat box. Some would be rattling off "hellos" to different screen names appearing in the chat box.

I'd heard the word id, and the concepts of id, ego and superego, but I didn't know what they meant and how they applied here. Id is the primitive and instinctive part of a personality. Id is the part focused on sex (eros) and death (thanatos). The death part is also aggression. Playing with camgirls online was pure id, because I was combining sexual stimulation with aggression (a stand-in for violence and death) in the messages I typed to them. I had no other outlet for my id, so it all went there. Subconsciously I used this sexual aggression to cope with losses.

The camgirls I liked ran the gamut. There was no consistent type of those I favored. These names are variations on what their screen names were. "Jade" looked like a Nordic blonde but spoke with a Spanish accent. She seemed aloof, like she wouldn't follow directions in private, but the one time I was with her, she surprised me by doing most of what I asked. "JessicaBad" had mousy brown curly hair, was skinny and tiny, and would talk dirty. I went private with her a couple times, but after a while, she changed the way she looked and my interest faded.

"Janice Boss" I went private with once or twice, but one of those times was especially notable, as I describe [elsewhere]. She had a punk rock or heavy metal style look – would be wearing hard rock themed t-shirts. Years later I stumbled on to a documentary about camgirls she was in, which shocked me because of that past connection I had to her. She had a superfan who was paying her tons of money on a regular basis, who even got her to fly to Australia to visit him.

As I watched, I envied this guy at first. As the story played out, it sunk in how obsessed this guy was. I could predict where it would go. The guy thought he might have a real relationship with Janice. She led him on for awhile, even saying she might get involved with him for real, but inevitably, she snapped out of that and disappointed him.

I remember other camgirls whose names I don't recall, but whose looks I do. One girl had a biker chick look, always in a leathery bikini with braided hair. Sometimes she wore pigtails suggesting innocence lost. She usually was good to me in private. There were others I got into but never went private with. One brunette sat in a feminine-looking bedroom, with pink walls, full of posters and knick-knacks. She had written "slut" with a marker on her belly, which was a giant turn-on, because it invited simulating sexual aggression.

In the free rooms, when I did have the nerve to type something, I'd go right to asking if the camgirls if they liked oral. It was my test of how well they would take direction if I went to private with them.

Angel & Devil 1

Around 2015, after midnight some nights at home, with my wife and child gone to sleep, I'd sit at my computer browsing camgirls. After Gabi caught me doing this, and we fought about it, she once said, trying to be kind to this lost soul, "Maybe we can look at them together."

"How would that work," I'd think to myself. Maybe I could do it. Could we be telling the girl what to do together? Would Gabi watch me as I did my usual thing?

Then in my mind I answer that question myself with a counterpoint.

--She wouldn't like it. She would be horrified watching what I do.

Eventually, Gabi would see what I did in privates anyway, and not in any way that brought her into it and made it something we shared together. I took to filming one I liked with my phone when she performed in private.

Gabi found that footage later, when my behavior pushed her to go through everything I was up to in my accounts.

In my mind, I justified my actions with the camgirls as not really cheating. I wasn't doing anything physical with anyone in the real world. I wasn't developing an emotional attachment to anyone. This was all just a sexual outlet.

But now I know it pulled my sexual preference completely away from my wife. Instead of thinking about going to bed with her at night, I'd try to wait until she went to bed alone, so I could be alone to check out cam-girls. I denied the reality that this sapped my interest in a sex life with my wife. And when we did have sex, I wasn't at all invested in her pleasure like I should have been.

Angel & Devil 2

Sometimes, years on into these habits, I'd try to cut back on the camgirls and just watch porn videos. The angel-and-devil arguments continued in my head as I strove to stick to recorded videos, not camgirl chats.

-I'll look at the camgirls to get worked up, but only that. … There's no one on now that I'm that into anyway. Maybe a couple who are familiar that I once tried but weren't satisfying.

-Ooh, Katarina is on tonight. I would explode with her, I want to direct her to be my 'slutty slave.'

-Why spend more right now? Just do the free stuff. They've got all the genres – blowjobs, bukakke, even JOI (jerk off instruction). You're into JOI lately.

-Just look over who's on one more time.

-Why? I'm ready to pop. Tired of waiting for the right one to turn up, or stay on and be free to chat. I'll watch the free videos.

That was the virtue versus vice tug of war in my head. I used to think just watching recorded footage was virtuous by comparison. I assumed or wanted to think that all the clips were women over 18 who appeared in them willingly. I suspended my disbelief that any of it could be the product of abuse, revenge porn, or worse. Once I read a news story about incidents like that, where the women never could get those videos completely scrubbed off the internet. Where one got taken down, it would pop back up someplace else or re-posted by someone else. The story said some of the women suffered depression and trauma from exposure like this—even suicide.

These videos and the women in them, go on and on entertaining guys using them to enhance masturbation, endlessly, in numbers in the thousands and millions, no doubt.

Lower East Side Vignette

Getting back to the real world, at times, I found social tribes where I fit. First in the improv classes and the UCB Theatre. Later, at a rock trivia night at Pianos on the Lower East Side.

For awhile, I went every Wednesday night I could. The subway ride of over an hour, from downtown to midtown and out deep into Queens, to get home late afterward wasn't a deterrent.

One time, after the event, I stayed on hanging out with the hosts and some of their friends. I'd gotten their attention by being so good at the games.

Having already had two beers during the trivia, I joined them all as they moved on to another bar and got more drinks. I tried to get close with one of the hosts, an attractive, tall rocker who worked in the music industry. She'd been talking with excitement about returning to the Bonnaroo Festival. I remember sitting next to her on barstools, letting my leg touch hers as we sat.

As drinkers might flow from one shiny object to another, we drifted apart – maybe she'd gone to talk to someone else, or maybe even I did. I found myself talking to another woman, a blonde who seemed to be hiding some pudginess under a sweatshirt and baggy clothes. There was something attractive to me about her too, and it wasn't just beer goggles.

We decide to take off from our crowd, stumble out of the bar together, to go to her place. She says she lives right nearby, but she has to move tomorrow. I'm a little baffled for a second that she's out doing what we're doing when she has to move the very next day, but I set that aside. We get to her apartment, which is a little studio walk-up in a five-story building. Going up the stairs starts to sober me up, and the conversation begins inside my head again.

-I don't know if I really dig this woman that much. Her apartment reeks of cigarette smoke. It feels grubby in here. But I'll try.

-You don't have to. This doesn't feel right.

-Go for it anyway.

She takes off her sweatshirt, exposing her busty chest in a plain grey bra, which I dig. I had been a little excited when she took off my pants, and we're kissing. I'm overlooking her smoky breath, but it starts getting to me.

The kissing moves to her bed and she's on her back. Instead of getting more aroused though, I'm starting to go soft. She notices. Then things take a turn.

--What is wrong with you? Are you gay or something?

--No. I don't know what's wrong, I say, stumbling through the words. I mumble that I'm tired.

I can see she's insulted. But the angel in my head has mercifully taken over. The devil walked out and abandoned this scene, since it's no longer looking like an easy hook-up. I pick up my pants and start putting them back on.

-Okay, go then, you asshole, she starts yelling at me. That sobers me up another degree. I can see that something is off about her mentally as she trains a lot of anger on me.

I mumble that I'm sorry.

-Take your 'sorry' and go. You're missing out, I would have fucked you really good.

At that point, I'm not even that disappointed anymore that it hasn't happened. I step toward the door, look back at her for a second, and go.

Mom Passes / Performing

Passing

In late 2013, I knew my mom was on her way out and it was just a matter of time. She'd been checked into hospice earlier in the week. Gabi and I had gone down to their house to visit, but Gabi took the train back to New York that morning. We had a tearful scene after visiting my mom together in the hospice the night before. Gabi told me later she just knew it would be the last time she'd see my mom.

After another hospice visit with my stepdad, followed by dinner, we returned to their house and went our separate ways. I must have stayed up for a while after he went to bed, maybe watching TV, then heading up to bed late after midnight.

In my teenage bedroom upstairs, the same one where I had a tiny TV and VCR for masturbation fodder in my early 20s, I had a little tablet computer with me. I pulled up the camgirls on it. I saw JaniceBoss was on and she usually didn't turn up that often. She was locked up in private sessions for a while, which sent me browsing around and working myself up, until the moment came that she was free and I could take her to private chat.

--Hey 'Studwood,' she greeted me, wearing a ripped up heavy metal band t-shirt, bikini bottoms and her bleached white rocker-style hair.

--Hey. Can you give me what I need tonight?

--Come pvt, baby.

--OK

--mmm, I want your mouth, I start off.

--how do you want it?

--my cock in it

--ooh, she types, pulling out a dildo and starting to lick it.

--yeah. I wanna see you drooly.

She starts to put it in her mouth.

--gag on me, I type.

She starts to oblige. By this point, I'm well into stroking myself, almost ready to grip it and pump. I'm lost, I'm so far gone.

It was right around this moment, 1:30 or 2 in the morning, down at the hospice 10 miles away, that my mom was expiring.

The camgirl entertains me to completion, I wipe off and I go to the bathroom and wipe off whatever I missed. Then back to the bedroom, I shut off the small table lamp and crash into sleep.

A couple hours later comes a knock on my bedroom door. Roused from sleep, I say, "come in." My stepdad opens the door, says "she's gone." I get up, still exhausted, and wrap him up in a big hug as he cries.

On that two hours sleep, I throw on some clothes, and drive us down to the hospice. The guard is expecting us. He leads us through a maze of hospital corridors. The hospice is a wing within a big hospital and they kept certain doors between the hospital and hospice locked after hours to ensure their separation. After several twists and turns, we get to the hall where my mom is and go in the room where she is serenely laid out on the bed. But her face is blank and I can feel that her soul is no longer there. My stepdad has gone in close to her for a few moments of saying goodbye and kissing her goodbye. Then I quietly do the same.

After that, it's all a blur. One thing after another. First, we sit down with the hospice staff and confirm instructions for the funeral home. A staff member tells us we should be on our way because we won't want to see mom wheeled out to be taken to the funeral home – that sight would be very upsetting.

Then, I drive us back to the house and sleep just a couple more hours. Then my stepdad and I are up again to go do the next tasks. Around 8 or 9 am—it's Saturday now—we go the funeral home. The undertaker tells us we need to clear out mom's safety deposit boxes right way, because once the banks are notified by the newspaper obituaries, they will lock those up for probate. And we don't get done with all the arrangements at the funeral home till about 11 am. Knowing banks have short hours on Saturday, I drive us in a frenzy to two different banks around town. We manage to clear everything out before their closing times of noon or 1 pm.

Then it's back home, to collapse into deep sleep again.

Performing

I've given a lot of thought to how I feel I behaved, in retrospect, as my mother was dying. I treated it as something to be hyper-conscious about, from how I acted while at the hospice to how I started writing what I would say at the funeral even before she passed. I figured that was OK because at that point, I knew it was inevitable and imminent.

This behavior, I feel now, was ridiculous. Even at that late date, there was still sibling rivalry with my sister. I saw that my sister couldn't even go up to our mother's room in the hospice until I got there for support. Maybe I wasn't consciously doing this, but I reacted to that by playing the hero, getting close and speaking thoughtfully with my mom, grandstanding in front of everyone else there – my sister, my wife and my stepdad.

Performing this way when a loved one is dying isn't denial, but once you recognize that's what happened, it feels regrettable and egotistical.

Lust in Friends Places

I liked crossword puzzles since I was a kid, subscribing to Games Magazine, where I learned acrostics. As an adult in New York, if I was out someplace Saturday night, I'd buy the early edition of the Sunday New York Times on my way home, because I got hooked on the Sunday crossword.

Before Moxie was born, I wasted tons of time playing games on Facebook – the ones designed to turn you into a rat constantly chasing cheese in an imaginary, virtual world, with ever increasing levels.

By the end of our daughter's first year, I was lost or burnt out, or both. Whatever it was, I got hooked on Words With Friends. At first I was only addicted to the game itself, until I twisted that into browsing opponents' pictures, looking for women who might chat with me.

This was different than looking at camgirls, of course, but it was still about sexual stimulation – trying

197

to find someone and some situation that would be new and exciting.

Sheila111 accepted my invite to play. Her picture wasn't especially pretty or sexy but still caught my eye. We played some games, and I started at first with very simple chat about the game play.

-Nice move, I wrote after she played a big word for a lot of points.

-Thank you ;), she writes back.

-;)

-This game's getting good ;)

-Oh yeah? How do you mean?

-I'm breaking a sweat.

-Are you getting wet?

-Play your next move, she tells me. And I do. I'm in the lead in points.

-Ooh, good one. I'm dripping.

-Beating you makes me hard.

I take the phone into the bathroom. I'm sitting on the toilet now.

-I better do something with that, she's written back.

-What are you gonna do? You're not gonna win.

-I'm gonna get you. I'm gonna ride that dick now. It's mine.

I'm stroking myself through my jeans. Then I'm taking it out of my pants, sitting there.

-Feel me throbbing hard, I text back.

-I'm gonna ride it so hard, I'm gonna break your dick in half.

That didn't turn me off. It got me more excited. It makes me start pumping with my hand.

This was not enough though. The next time I engage in a word game with her, I get her email and ask her for pictures. She sends me a couple she took in what looks like a bathroom steamed up by a running hot shower, with her wrapped in just a towel.

After a couple of these emails, things change abruptly. She stops responding to moves in the game, and when I persist with flirting in the game, she writes back, I've been thinking...

...this stuff is wrong. I don't want to keep doing this, she says.

It's a wake-up call to me, because I knew this was wrong but was doing it anyway. I just could not stop being suggestive and dirty through the game, with anyone who would reciprocate. Many brushed it off, but there were a couple or a few who entertained it, although not nearly as much as sheila111.

After that, we still played an occasional game, but without writing anything in the chat, until eventually that faded out too. This cyber affair ended a year or two before my wife uncovered the evidence of it.

Found Out

I stand in the shallow end of the Olympic size indoor pool, about 20 feet away from the side. I'm holding onto our two-and-a-half-year-old daughter in her floating tube raft. Kids are buzzing all around us in the pool. Most of them are several years older than our daughter, here for my friend's son's birthday party. One boy is right on top of us doting on our daughter, bombarding me with comments and questions, which makes me tense.

Coping with that stimulus right in front of me, I also spot my wife in the bleachers in the middle distance. She'd been holding up my phone, with its distinctive red case, to take pictures of us in the pool. After she's taken a few shots, I then see her browsing the phone and starting to look more and more dismayed. Immediately, I know she's found something bad that will be a problem.

About half hour later, we emerge from the locker room, changed back into street clothes.

201

"I wanna talk to you about what's on here," she says, holding my phone.

"Let me have it," I say, grabbing the phone out of her hand. I head off with it down the hall, away from everyone – leaving our daughter with her without a word.

I wander into the empty gym and sit down with the phone, deleting the gaming app I'd been using to chat with women. "Why does she have to dig into this?" I think to myself, angry.

Consequences

It had been a miserable day, of my own making, but I still took it as a punishment and misery being inflicted on me. Gabi and I argued in the guest bedroom of my friend's house as we packed for what was supposed to be our romantic night in a hotel, while our daughter would stay with the friends.

-Keep it down, I say. I don't want them to hear anything about what's going on with us. Do you?

-No, I don't, she say. But I could kill you right now.

She's torn between whether to indeed kill me or at least leave me, or try to enjoy a night together when the chances to have one of those were so rare.

-So if you don't want it out in the open, then quiet down, I say.

-If you said that in any other place, I'd throttle you, she replies. Then quietly seethes as we finish packing a bag for one night.

Taking cold comfort that she won't air my failing in front of the friend, we drive about 30 minutes to the hotel, with neither of us saying a word. We get there, check in and get dressed for a nice dinner out like we'd planned. Over the time she's in the bathroom and out of my sight, I relax a bit from the tension between us up to that point. I wonder if I should tell the friends what's happened, and the inner debate bubbles up.

-It's not even all revealed yet, I think.

-But it eventually will be. She will have to dig into all your stuff, and you know that.

-Why does she insist on having to know about this? It's not real cheating anyway, it wasn't in person.

-She can't see it that way.

-Well, she will, and what are you going to do about it?

-I need help. Maybe my friends will understand?

-Are you crazy? Your newer friends from the city aren't even dating anybody, and your married friend here would definitely disapprove.

-I guess you're right. I wish he'd understand, but I can't imagine he'd be sympathetic.

Years later, that friend couldn't even be supportive or understand when my wife and I, somewhat healed and united, were fighting against financial misfortune. So my fracturing the marriage would have been completely unacceptable to these friends. I don't think they would have had my back – if they were judgmental about a financial failing, it would have been more so with a moral failing.

The devil's advocate inside my head continued, insisting on driving home his point.

-This is a guy who's been married for over 15 years and was engaged before online dating even really existed. Maybe he looks at porn in his basement, but it's probably far tamer than the shit you got into.

-You're probably right.

-He would scold you. He'll say he likes to look at girlie pictures or the young girls around his workplace, but even that carries an undercurrent of condescension toward any guy who would go further than that. You know he would never even so much as flirt with those girls.

-O.K., O.K., I get it. I'll just keep it all inside and buttoned up. I guess I should only share this with a therapist anyway.

* * *

We're back at home a few days after the pool incident opened the floodgates of my dishonesty. Our daughter is asleep.

--I know you took it off your phone, she says. Where are the messages from Words With Friends? I will find everything. Who's this "dirtysheila111"?

At this point, the barrage of uncovering my illicit online trail has worn away my denials. But I'm still not contrite enough to give away anything that she doesn't know or hasn't found.

--Someone I wrote to, I say, knowing that will read as an admission of some sort, at least. I won't connect the dots between that email handle and the one I sexted with on Words With Friends.

In shame, and still trying to stay in denial, I avoid looking at her, just listening to her detective work and questions, responding as little as possible. She continues going through my computer files.

--Play this video, she commands. It's the one where I filmed a camgirl. My stomach sinks. She's over my shoulder watching it, and watching me as it plays. No longer a source of gratification, the video has become mortifying and shameful.

Bloomingdale's, December 2018

I climb the stairs from the 4/5 train at 59th and Lexington to a set of glass doors that lead right into the sub-basement "Metro" level of Bloomingdale's. This department store, a New York institution, was important enough to be linked right into the transit system. It's before the store opens at 10 a.m. and I show my employee badge to the guard seated just inside the doors.

I'm feeling fried from the argument with my wife the night before because I relapsed. I hadn't completely banished that tendency. I was sexting to my favorite camgirl and couldn't shut the phone before she took it and read what I wrote. I'm in a rush to get all the way up to the 10th floor employee area to put my stuff in a locker and prepare to face a crush of holiday customers in men's accessories, where I worked part-time. Sometimes this might require two different elevators, which didn't help my anxiousness about being on time.

Making this journey began through those glass doors, then weaved through displays of hip-hop clothes to an escalator that went up just one level to the elevator bank. At least when customers weren't in the store yet, it was easier to catch a direct elevator to the 10th floor. Most of the cars stopped on the ninth floor and then you'd have to take the stairs.

Once on 10, I'd hang my coat. This also was easier before a day's opening because there would be some open hangers still. The bag I always carried because I had to have stuff on me for breaks went into a temporary locker where you'd have to make a combination on the spot. In my rush, sometimes I'd either forget the combination or couldn't remember which locker I'd used. When realizing that later at break times, you'd have to go get help from store security.

I had still more steps after that – then going to an employee bathroom in the back hallways to neaten up after the trip in, until I was finally ready to go back down to the first floor where I worked. Stepping out of those iconic elevators, I'd walk at a brisk pace toward the 3rd Avenue side of the store, past cosmetic counters on my right, then the employee entrance and "Gallery" boutique space on my left. Usually I'd quickly glance at the Gallery space which had artsier displays and an unusual assortment of products that could include a reissued version of Polaroid cameras, the Beastie Boys coffee table book, and Sharper Image-type gadgets.

Among the cosmetic counters, I'd often see a tall, thin Eastern European woman, in her early 40s. She wore high heels, tight dresses and bright makeup. She had bleached blonde curly hair tied up in a messy bun. She towered over all the other young women working in men's fragrances. I wondered what her story was – she must have had an interesting one – or what her deal was. I assumed she was very high maintenance with anyone and everyone.

After that, I'd arrive at the back hallway of the store, paralleling 3rd Avenue, that they called the Men's Arcade. Turning left took me to the two counters where I most often worked. Turning right, I'd pass sections for Prada men's accessories, MCM bags and accessories (popular in hip-hop fashion) and various men's luggage pieces.

The counters where I worked sat across from each other, with one surrounded by Burberry accessories and the other being a wrap-around counter with displays of watches, wallets and cufflinks. That one also had Shinola watches and wallets, a retro brand that I came to like. The walls around that counter had Tumi bags and overpriced electronic goods including Beats headphones – at prices higher than just about any other retailer. When I started, I knew nothing about most of these brands and items— probably hadn't heard of some of the brands. As I worked there, I learned to pretend like I knew something about all of it.

When the store opened its doors in the morning, Frank Sinatra's "New York, New York," played on the sound system throughout. Every time the song hit its booming refrain, "If I can make it there/I'll make it anywhere," it stung. Here I was working in a department store, having clearly not "made it," to help support my family – the same family where I was currently in the doghouse, where I deserved to be.

I looked forward to days when I knew Murray was working, an older gentleman and quite a character. I have poor gay-dar, so I didn't figure out his orientation for awhile. In a previous career-track job, I didn't figure out that my bosses were a couple for at least a year. I can be that clueless.

Normally, I looked forward to bantering with Murray, but today it hurt to put on a happy face and pretend everything was alright with me. My mind was filled with how awful things were with my wife. Filled with dread of how it would be when I returned home after work.

I was never one for big gifts or flowers, and my wife had become resigned to that disappointment. Sheepish in my own mind, I thought I could and should come home with something. A big gift or giant bouquet of flowers would be over the top. That wasn't like me, and something extravagant would seem insincere, I thought.

It hit me. Gabi knew about the Magnolia Bakery having a store within Bloomingdale's and she always appreciated a gourmet cupcake. I could bring a couple of them home for her. That would be sincere, nice but not too crazy or overcompensating. I was doing a double shift and had to check when the bakery closed. I wanted to get the freshest cupcake I could, and stash it somewhere till my shift was done.

Later, tired, I exit the train at my home stop in Forest Hills, Queens. I'm in my thick coat, wearing my backpack, carrying a small box from Magnolia. Queens Boulevard, where I emerge from the train, is not well lit like midtown Manhattan outside the store. By work, the sky only appears dark way up high past the tall buildings. In the boroughs, the darkness is a lot closer to the ground.

I'm spent from the workday, being on my feet for hours on end. I'd sometimes get sore feet from the dress shoes I wore there. I knew that bringing home a cupcake was just a fearful way to see if she was receptive to forgiving me, without actually asking.

Climbing up the stairs to home, my defensive posture kicked in as I put the key in the lock. Gabi's sitting on the couch watching TV. I ask in a measured voice, is Moxie already in bed.

-Yes, she says.

I take the bakery box out of my bag.

She's puzzled for a brief moment. Then I see her remember what happened the night before and put it together why I've brought her something now. Long accustomed to a lack of romantic demonstrations, she does recognize this meager gesture as my olive branch to her.

She saw the box with the single cupcake and knew it was for her and quietly smiled. "You got my favorite. This doesn't just make it all go away, but this is appreciated."

She knew I was tired from my day, but she later shared that it would have been nice if I'd followed up with something that took more effort than going to the bakery in the same building — like a letter or hand-picked flowers. It wasn't the cost, but the effort that mattered to her, especially after everything that happened.

The fears and the flaws were far from worked out yet, but this was the first inkling that they could be.

Nightcrawler

My job at Bloomingdale's ended out of necessity. We decided to move out of New York for a fresh start in suburban New Jersey, not far from where I grew up. It was another step in a protracted humiliation from losing a job, fucking up our marriage, going bankrupt and struggling financially. I needed to earn income by any means I could. I was doing that with Bloomingdale's, but out in New Jersey I turned to food delivery apps. I learned to have a few different ones running at the same time, to get all possible orders out there, and as I kept doing it, I got better at it, choosing and grouping together ones in close locations.

I'd eat dinner early so I could go out around 6 pm for three or four hours and catch the dinner rush business. The money was nothing compared to what I could make from freelance writing. A really great night on the apps might gross about $100. But it was still $100 more than I would have had.

I got more efficient and more strategic, choosing orders from restaurants and fast food places along Route 1. I could pick up two or three then set out to deliver them, hoping the destinations were close enough together that it wouldn't lead to complaints about late deliveries. Inevitably, delivery destinations didn't line up well every time. A couple times, I got speeding tickets trying to keep up. Customers could call me through the apps and check on me. If I was juggling too much I wouldn't even pick up those calls. If I did pick up, I'd shut them down by immediately saying something like, "it's busy and there's a lot of orders tonight."

Fielding those calls increased my perception of the customers as spoiled, too lazy to go get food themselves and so entitled they were calling about a delivery just 10 or 15 minutes late. The worst orders were ones from private boarding schools – Lawrenceville School, Hun School and Peddie School. It's satisfying to call them out for the spoiled brats they were. I'd end up having to call them when I got there. These kids couldn't even give directions for how to find their dorm on campus. They couldn't even figure out how to tell anyone a spot to meet them. They would murmur and give vague and confused instructions that didn't make sense. Before too long, I'd avoid their orders unless it was really slow. If I realized that I'd accepted an order going to these schools, I'd drop the order or give it back to the pool—unless it was really slow going.

Colleges were no picnic either. Princeton University was slightly better than the rest because the GPS actually registered specific campus buildings and could get you there, which never worked with the boarding schools. Rider University was just as bad as those private high schools. These weren't rich kids, but their campus buildings didn't show up as separate locations on a GPS either. Also, Rider students were just as bad at directing you to their dorm or wherever they were. It wasn't that they were entitled, it was more like they weren't bright enough to know how to direct a delivery driver to where they were.

But it wasn't all bad. It got me out for the evening, even if my depression wasn't helped by knowing I had to do this work. Still, it was rewiring my brain. The effort to figure out logistics for picking up multiple orders at once and then getting them all delivered in succession made me aggressive at the wheel. That wired aggression lasted a while after I stopped for the night.

Delivery apps brought out my competitive nature. At the end of each Bloomingdale's shift, you could print out the value of how much you'd rung up in purchases. I got a kick out of seeing a big number. My best day was during the Christmas holidays where I topped $6,000 in a shift. A good regular shift was about $1,000. Over the eight or nine months I was there, I had a few thousand dollars' worth in sales several times.

The difference with the delivery apps is that it was more concrete – it was about what I actually going to earn. If I earned a big number for the night, I'd feel good.

The delivery apps also had other effects on my mental wiring. Alone in my car in the dark, I'd live for a moment where a sexy woman might answer the door for delivery.

This was rare, but it did happen. Once I delivered to a doorway down an alley in Princeton across from the university. It must have been the entrance to an apartment up the stairs. A young Indian girl came down the stairs in a negligee, on a cold night, and answered the door and took the food. I wasn't so deluded as to think this had anything to do with me. She just hadn't cared about modesty while grabbing the food order. This one was just a funny story I could tell. But it made me think about the possibilities of being creepy while doing this work. It crossed my mind, but stayed in the realm of just thoughts.

That didn't stop sexual daydreams in the car as I drove and delivered. In the hills of Princeton, way north of the school, I drove a delivery down a dark road that led to a turn down another even darker and more secluded road. This road led to a big yellow house that was the destination. Floodlights lit up the left side of the house and its long driveway to the porch, while the right side of the house sat in the dark. Lights in the windows were low. The differences in lighting made the whole setting feel strange to me.

A young woman with long dirty blonde hair, wearing baggy sweats, answered the door. Even the casual clothes couldn't hide her plain, un-made up attractiveness. I was polite. She tipped some cash, which rarely happened. I didn't hear any other voices or activity coming from behind her in the house. It seemed like she was all alone in this isolated residence.

A few weeks later, I had a delivery in the same general area, and realized I was pulling up to that same house. The young woman seemed to be the only one there again. I started to wonder what her story was. Was she housesitting? Was she a trust fund baby in this big spacious house? She didn't seem old enough or seasoned enough to have owned this house on her own. Someone young and wealthy would rather be in an apartment in a city, I'd assume.

As I walked back to my car, I started fantasizing about what it would be like to make a move on her. I would never have done that, because I'd gotten past the urge to cheat, not to mention how creepy and wrong it would have been. The thoughts still bounced around in my head, though:

-My god, she's all alone up here. I just know it. What if I paid her a compliment?

-You know you want to do more than that.

-It would be so hot to just go up to her, grab her and kiss her. What if she was receptive? She could be, all alone like that.

-Or, she could kick you in the balls. I know you're fantasizing about her immediately giving in.

-Yeah. Or I could tell her she can call me when she wants something delivered.

-So, you're going to drop everything at any time if she texted you to pick up food for her? How would you explain that exactly, genius? Are you insane?

-Yeah, you're right, I am insane. Oh well.

-I thought so.

-It's so exciting to think about.

-I know. But still. Just keep that in your head and to yourself.

-Yeah, alright.

After clamping down on this twisted fantasy and thinking about the reality of the situation, it knocked my ego down a few more pegs. I was an older guy, down on his luck, delivering food to a young woman with more potential who'd likely get further in life than I had. A lyric from the Who's "The Real Me" stuck in my head – "the girl I once loved, lives in this yellow house. ... she don't wanna know me now; can you see the real me..."

The net result of times like this was a downer. Other instances, for no sensible reason, also affected me that way. I also delivered to a lot of hotel rooms in the area. Those were usually great because they would tip more and it was simple and easy to find their location. One night, though, as I walked through the lobby of a large higher-end hotel, I realized that the ballroom I just passed was the location of my high school prom. That realization knocked the wind out of me. I remembered the high school kid I was, with all his grand aspirations. Yet here I was in the exact same spot so many years later, doing the work that a failure does.

Fortunately, more freelance work kicked in again, and just before the Covid pandemic lockdowns began, I'd bowed out of delivery work.

Catalysts

Covid changed a lot for everyone. Even with the stray fantasies I had while out hustling with the food delivery apps, I was on a road to atonement, but after months of lockdown, I gained more perspective about marriage. Around September 2020, a quiet epiphany struck me. The ways I had been wrong truly sunk in and I began to open up to how I should act from then on. I had to learn or re-learn how to love my wife and be true.

Just before the lockdown, there were some issues with Mark, that closest longtime friend, who appears in some of the formative experiences from my teens and 20s shared in this book. I'd see him from time to time, even coming down from New York for visits, and I'd complain about our marriage to him, dumping a lot on him. He'd listen but I don't think he was that sympathetic to my troubles. A long, long time ago, we'd become very different people than we were when we first became friends. Out of loyalty to that past, I kept the friendship going when it might have otherwise quietly receded over time. I was willfully blind to these differences and the lack of support that a true friendship should have.

In short, there was a clash in personalities between our wives. My wife and I felt resentment and hurt about a lack of understanding of the financial and other pressures on us. One night that caused us to back out from attending one of their sons' school play at the last minute. This blew everything up. It led to me pulling completely away from him for almost two years.

It wasn't easy to let go of that friendship, or at least stop holding it in such high regard, and I had to be sure I was confident in the reasons, some of which my wife did help me see. And that was about more than just a spouse who doesn't like one of their spouse's friends badmouthing that friend all the time. She made a substantive case.

I would have to be OK with my choice to pull away from that friend. I am still on friendly terms with him, but I no longer give that such high importance in my life.

The Battle Inside My Head

Writing this memoir began in earnest following those conclusions in fall 2020. By March or April of 2021, the writing became a struggle. To kick-start ideas and thoughts again, I began pouring through psychologists' writing about sex addiction, from both those who believe it's real and those who say it's not genuine. I needed to understand what sex addiction was about either way and figure out what I thought and where I stood.

I vacillated on this question as I compared my experiences and actions to the views in everything I was reading. Going in, I leaned toward the assertion that I was a sex addict in the way I interacted with porn and camgirls.

Then I would read David Ley, a clinical psychologist who wrote that there is no such thing as sex addiction. But he didn't cast sex addiction as an excuse for bad behavior. This seemed like splitting hairs or trying to walk both sides of a fine line.

In the end, after all my reading, I still felt like the addiction was real – but it shouldn't be an excuse – that I could still fight the addiction and get free of it. The opposing view, that sex addiction isn't real, could justify my actions as OK, and just an aspect of life. That opposing view, one I probably subscribed to at times, didn't sit right with me anymore. If the addiction is real, like I've concluded, that raises another question. Should it be forgiven? That depends on what I have done about it and am I genuinely – have I genuinely – addressing it.

So how did I get to this point? As I thought about that question, again I had dueling voices in my head. There are cultural theories, psychological theories, sociological commentary and activism all debating the idea of sex addiction, as well as how society should treat pornography. Out of all of that, what makes sense to me?

There's plenty of evidence that I was indeed addicted. On top of that, I was trying to keep it all a secret, as addicts do. That affected my enthusiasm for everything else in life – career, marriage, parenting and friendships.

For a long time, I could not muster up real power to fight the addiction. The way I developed as a child and a teenager made me more susceptible to the path of a sex addiction. Yet I couldn't blame that forever.

What I became was inescapable, based both on background and on choices. Staying that way didn't have to be inescapable.

Angel & Devil 3

It took all these decades to reconcile all these issues and get to a better place. The devilish libido still can climb up on my shoulder and say:

--It would be so hot to indulge just once. It doesn't mean you don't love your wife or appreciate her.

The angel steps in.

--You don't need the gratification. You truly can be fine without it. You've been showing that.

The devil rebuts.

--It would just be a momentary lapse. You can do it, file it away and get back to normal.

The angel says,

--You can't get back to normal completely from it. You never could. This urge is the pain of the past. It's a gut reaction to all the rejections, and that's all it is. Here's the great thing – the sweetest thing -- you aren't being rejected now.

Epilogue

When I look back at photos and videos from throughout our marriage and raising our daughter, I'm sometimes surprised by all the laughing and joking I see. These times most likely happened even when I was at my worst as an addict or even when the marriage was strained to almost the breaking point.

In couples therapy, when we're asked what we have in common, Gabi will often say, "we laugh a lot together."

After being married 12 years, and having known each other nearly 15 years, that's the one constant we have. I know her more intimately than I could know any audience. My wit is the quickest it can be when I'm trying to be funny – it doesn't even feel like trying, like I have to get over any obstacle to come up with something Gabi laughs at.

The things I did online, the way I strayed in marriage, sparked tons of fights. Many of these might have seemed to be about other subjects but all of them were rooted in the tensions between us. Our daughter was young, and she may not have understood whatever subject matter she heard, but at formative ages of 2 through 4, she had to absorb a lot of this tension. It's possible she has a lot of subconscious resentment and anger at me already because of this. She may not realize it or understand why. I can't fix this or change this now. It's a great regret in my life, maybe the greatest regret of all, because I can perceive this lingering damage. All I can do is try to be better and to be there for her. I'm always going to be atoning for it, and that's the way it should be. I can't ever forget that.

Thanks:

Gabi – for patience, understanding and staying

*   *   *

Kevin Allison – for storytelling coaching that help me find
my way in writing this memoir.

Jen Braaksma – helping fine-tune the storytelling
Chris Gethard – "Lose Well" gave me the final push I
needed to make this book happen.

New York City – the laboratory and the crucible that
made me who I am now.

*   *   *

Acknowledgements:

Ken Krantz & Chip Chantry of "I Love Rock and Roll" podcast,
John Shea, and to the exes I hurt, I'm sorry.

*   *   *

Inspirations:

Marc Maron, Peter Gabriel, James Ellroy

Design, layout and cover by Natalia Junqueira